Rosenfeld in Retrospect

Rosenfeld in Retrospect presents original psychoanalytic papers showing the influence of Herbert Rosenfeld on psychoanalysis today, and reproduces some of Rosenfeld's most important clinical writings.

In the first part of this book, *The conference papers: contemporary developments of Rosenfeld's work*, the editor brings together papers and discussions by Rosenfeld's well-known contemporaries, Ronald Britton, Michael Feldman, Edna O'Shaughnessy, Hanna Segal and Riccardo Steiner who explore his contribution to psychoanalysis. John Steiner demonstrates the importance of Rosenfeld's classic papers, and critically surveys the more controversial developments in his later work. The second part contains four papers by Rosenfeld, chosen by his colleagues to be his most significant and original contributions.

This collection conveys Rosenfeld's liveliness and influence, and will be of interest to all of those attracted to his work.

John Steiner is a training analyst of the British Psychoanalytical Society and works in private practice as a psychoanalyst. He is the author of several psychoanalytic papers and the book *Psychic Retreats*.

Rosenfeld in Retrospect

Essays on his clinical influence

Edited by John Steiner

Routledge
Taylor & Francis Group

LONDON AND NEW YORK

First published 2008
by Routledge
27 Church Road, Hove, East Sussex BN3 2FA

Simultaneously published in the USA and Canada
by Routledge
270 Madison Avenue, New York NY 10016

Reprinted 2009

Routledge is an imprint of the Taylor & Francis Group, an Informa business

Typeset in Times by Garfield Morgan, Swansea, West Glamorgan
Printed and bound in Great Britain by the MPG Books Group
Paperback cover design by Andy Ward

This publication has been produced with paper manufactured to strict
environmental standards and with pulp derived from sustainable forests.

British Library Cataloguing in Publication Data
A catalogue record for this book is available from the British Library

Library of Congress Cataloging in Publication Data
Rosenfeld in retrospect : essays on his clinical influence / edited by John
Steiner.
    p. ; cm.
  Includes bibliographical references and index.
  ISBN 978-0-415-46114-6 (hbk) — ISBN 978-0-415-46115-3 (pbk.) 1.
Rosenfeld, Herbert A. 2. Psychoanalysis. 3. Narcissism. I. Steiner, John, 1934-
II. Rosenfeld, Herbert A.
  [DNLM: 1. Rosenfeld, Herbert A. 2. Psychoanalysis. 3. Narcissism—
Collected Works. 4. Narcissism. 5. Psychoanalysis—Collected Works. 6.
Psychoanalytic Therapy—Collected Works. 7. Psychoanalytic Therapy. WM
460 R8183 2008]
  RC504.R594 2008
  616.89'17—dc22

                                                              2007044029

ISBN: 978-0-415-46114-6 (hbk)
ISBN: 978-0-415-46115-3 (pbk)

Contents

List of contributors

Ronald Britton was educated at the Royal Grammar School Lancaster and University College London; he qualified in Medicine at University College Hospital in 1956, and is a Fellow of the Royal College of Psychiatrists. He is a training analyst of the Institute of Psychoanalysis and was formerly Chair of the Child and Family Dept Tavistock Clinic, President of the British Psychoanalytic Society and a Vice-President of the International Psychoanalytic Association.

Michael Feldman is a training and supervising analyst of the British Psychoanalytical Society. In addition to his clinical work and teaching in London, he regularly works with analysts in several European countries, and the USA. His papers explore theoretical and technical issues that arise in the interplay of transference and counter-transference, the patient's use of projective mechanisms, and the pressures both on the patient and the analyst towards defensive action rather than thought. He has co-edited, with Elizabeth Bott Spillius, *Psychic Equilibrium and Psychic Change: Selected Papers of Betty Joseph* (Routledge, 1989).

Edna O'Shaughnessy is a training analyst for children and adults in the British Psychoanalytical Society. Her many papers include 'Enclaves and Excursions', 'What is a Clinical Fact?', 'Relating to the Super-ego' and 'Whose Bion?'

Hanna Segal is one of the most important figures in British psychoanalysis. Her first book, *An Introduction to the Work of Melanie Klein*, has become a classic and she has since written four more books and a large number of original papers in psychoanalysis including several on the psychoanalytical contribution to aesthetics and to the sociopolitical field. She has twice served as President of the British Psychoanalytical Society and as Vice-President of the International Psychoanalytic Association. Her latest book, *Yesterday, Today and Tomorrow* was published in 2007.

John Steiner is a training analyst of the British Psychoanalytical Society and works in private practice as a psychoanalyst. He is the author of several psychoanalytic papers and the book *Psychic Retreats*.

Riccardo Steiner is the author of several papers and books including important work on the history of psychoanalysis. His account, with Pearl King, of the Controversial Discussions in the British Society has won special acclaim. He is a psychoanalyst in private practice and a member of the British Psychoanalytical Society.

Acknowledgements

I would like to thank:

The Melanie Klein Trust for their support and for permission to use the papers from the conference sponsored by the Trust on the work of Herbert Rosenfeld held in April 2000.

The *International Journal of Psychoanalysis* for permission to republish Chapter 7, Analysis of a schizophrenic state with depersonalisation (1947), Chapter 8, On the psychopathology of narcissism: a clinical approach (1964) and Chapter 9, A clinical approach to the psychoanalytic theory of the life and death instincts: an investigation into the aggressive aspects of narcissism (1971).

Angela Rosenfeld, Executor for the work of Dr H.A Rosenfeld for permission to republish Chapter 10, Contributions to the psychopathology of Psychotic Patients. The importance of projective identification in the ego structure and object relations of the psychotic patient (1971). Also for her help and support with both the conference and the book.

I would also like to offer thanks to the authors of the chapters and in particular to Dr Michael Feldman, Dr Ron Britton, Mrs Edna O'Shaughnessy, Dr Hanna Segal and Miss Betty Joseph who read parts of the manuscript and helped me to choose the papers by Rosenfeld which appear here.

The photograph of the bust by the Brazilian sculptor Christina Motta was taken by Dr Michael Feldman.

Introduction

John Steiner

In April 2000 the Melanie Klein Trust sponsored a conference on the work of Herbert Rosenfeld, and the enthusiasm generated on that day led to the decision to bring out this book. Its aim was to keep alive an interest in his work and to show how it has influenced a contemporary approach. It was clear that such a conference cannot give a comprehensive overview, and this has to await a scholarly appraisal of his contribution, but in editing the book I did hope to give a flavour of his achievement and to remind colleagues of his importance, particularly since, at least in my view, he is currently undervalued. Certainly many of his former students and colleagues see him as one of the most influential of those analysts who were students of Melanie Klein and who applied and extended her ideas.

In keeping with the aim of conveying his liveliness and influence I decided to present the papers from the conference with only minor editorial amendments.[1] This is particularly evident in the paper by Riccardo Steiner but is true for the other papers where the text and comments of the discussants seem to me to deepen and enliven the themes just as his own work did.

Part I contains the three conference papers by Mrs Edna O'Shaughnessy, Dr Ron Britton and Professor Riccardo Steiner, and the discussions by Dr Michael Feldman and Dr Hanna Segal. Following these I have included a review of Rosenfeld's work which I wrote after the conference was over. In this account I try to demonstrate the importance of his classic papers and I also attempt a critical survey of some of the more controversial developments in his later work.

Part II consists of four papers by Rosenfeld himself, which were chosen after a good deal of discussion with colleagues. We were clearly not able to be comprehensive or balanced and went instead for what we thought were his most significant and original contributions.

Throughout the book I have tried to avoid sexist language, but I sometimes use 'he' to refer to the analyst or patient of either sex for the sake of simplicity and clarity.

All the authors in this book knew Rosenfeld personally and all of them have, in different ways, been influenced by him, so that the book as a whole is an individual rather than an academic account of his work. We hope that the readers will be able to use it as an introduction to some of his best work and that they will be stimulated to read further for themselves and come to their own appraisal of the work of a major contributor to psychoanalysis.

Part I

The conference papers

Contemporary developments of Rosenfeld's work

Chapter 1

Intrusions

Edna O'Shaughnessy

In the first paper in his book *Psychotic States*, Rosenfeld writes of a patient that her 'central anxiety was a fantasy of the persecuting analyst forcing himself into her to control her and rob her, not only of her inner possessions, for instance, her babies and her feelings, but her very self (1947: 22). Persecutory anxieties about an invading analyst, following on the patient's phantasies of intrusion, is a theme that runs through Rosenfeld's pioneering papers of the forties, fifties and sixties. He describes the whole syndrome: the infantile anxiety and greed that impels the intrusion, the new identity the patient obtains by this type of projective identification, which carries with it fears of ego-disintegration in addition to anxieties of being trapped in and confused with the object, and how, in order to keep the analyst out, the patient does not speak about events that might arouse interest, withdraws and negates interpretations. If these things are now not new, it is because Rosenfeld, foremost among others, made them familiar.

At the time Rosenfeld was writing these papers Melanie Klein was still alive. 'Notes on Some Schizoid Mechanisms', where she named projective identification, appeared in 1946, and *Envy and Gratitude* in 1957. These works greatly influenced Rosenfeld, as they did all who followed Klein's new thinking. It was a time of fertile Kleinian development. Rosenfeld was investigating psychoanalysis as a treatment for schizophrenic and severe borderline patients, as were others, notably Bion and Segal. Bion proposed new hypotheses about the psychotic personality and Segal made the important differentiation between symbols and symbolic equations – both areas in which Rosenfeld also made contributions. He focused on the impairment of the psychotic ego, not from Bion's angle of the fragmentation and projection of the ego to form bizarre objects, but from the perspective of the impairment of the ego that results from an intrusion into the object, also the angle from which he approached the loss of symbolic functioning. He writes for instance

> whenever verbal contact was disturbed, through the patient's difficulty in understanding words as symbols, I observed that his phantasies of

going into me and being inside me had become intensified . . . For it is the quantity of the self involved in the process of projective identification that determines whether the real object and its symbolic representation can be differentiated.

(Rosenfeld 1952: 77)

Rosenfeld is here making an important clinical point: there are degrees of intrusion into the object; intrusion is not always 'all the way'.

As we know, Herbert Rosenfeld has had a huge influence. John Steiner's (1989) essay records the wealth of observations and measured assessments and the original conceptualisations that are to be found in Rosenfeld's papers. Rosenfeld was not afraid of mental illness and he eschewed what a patient of his called 'the bluff' – the bluff of transference peace. He had an extraordinary capacity to be where ill patients were, in schizoid, manic and depressed places, to understand their compressed utterances and interpret in strong plain words, often making what he called an 'integrative interpretation' of their total situation.

Rosenfeld's work on intrusions into the object, i.e. invasive projective identification, is invaluable when trying to work with patients like Mr B, who omnipotently take themselves into the analyst, mostly not going all the way, so that they are in, and at the same time out of, the analyst.

Mr B came for analysis in a desperate state. He was depressed and anxious and complained he had no memories of his parents, both dead, and that he was insecure about his gender. From the start he was in a double world. He tried to talk and to listen, and at the same time was anxious he was in a void and just as anxious that I might communicate with him dangerously so that he quickly withdrew, sometimes into sleep. What he managed to hear he was cautious about, often detaching it from me, so gaining 'pieces of knowledge'. Our verbal contact was anyway thin and experiences of communicating to me and being understood were weakly internalised. To protect himself from his huge anxiety Mr B gave most of his attention to sensations: of snuggling into a soft place, of feeling himself to be a girl with breasts, or feeling remote like a superior phallus. Sometimes his sensation world collapsed into being only a lavatory world of urine and faeces.

These sensations were based on projective identifications consequent on omnipotent phantasies of intrusion that began before his session. Mr B arrived early in my vicinity, concretely for him the psychoanalysis area; he went into the Heath for a walk to the pond, and then came out of the Heath to walk to my house for his session, where, in another mode, he repeated his two journeys. On first seeing me, unable to wait or stay separate, he went omnipotently inside me with his eyes, and then on the couch some of him came back with anxiety to the reality of being outside. The phantasies of being inside were idealised as offering a pleasurable 'other reality' that was meant to free him from unwelcome knowledge and all anxiety. However, they never quite succeeded in freeing him from anxieties of entrapment, weakness of self, of being watched and disparaged by a pathological super-ego and, in addition, of a pervasive guilt about withdrawing and keeping me out.

Thus, objects entered Mr B's mind in an imbalanced way: incorporations that followed upon his projective identifications predominated over identifications that were a sequel to introjections, with the result that Mr B enacted identities, acting out and 'in', far more than he was mentally active. Segal (1991) has examined the opposition – so significant for clinical work – between acting out and mental action.

Freud (1911) describes the 'momentous step' of the setting up of the reality principle as requiring a heightened awareness of attention and memory, a system of notation, and a passing of judgement to decide whether a notion is true or false. All these ego functions were interfered with – I think from a young age – by Mr B's divided way of being which distorted his relation to reality. His attention is largely engrossed with a sexualised watching of his objects' insides, so that his notation is predominantly from a sex and bottom world that he 'sees' in his voyeuristic phantasies. Feeding might be noted as shitting, talking misconceived as sex, and so on, and he makes no assessment of the truth or falsity of these confabulations. John Steiner describes how 'in most retreats reality is neither fully accepted nor completely disavowed' (1993: 88), which was exactly so with my patient. Steiner's theory of psychic retreats (1993) which is based on Rosenfeld's theory of narcissistic organisations has been of much help in trying to understand Mr B.

It was difficult to make contact with Mr B. I had to take account of the variations in his capacity for symbolic thinking and not miss his meagre attempts at communication which came almost unaccompanied by emotional projections, all the while being provoked and pressured by Mr B to involve myself with the details of his erotised sensations and phantasies. Had I done this last, it would have been, in Rosenfeld's phrase, to 'lose my very self'. Despite Mr B's annoyed protests that I kept ignoring his gender problems, I focused not on their details but on their invasiveness and function.

At first my main focus was on their defensive function, against the anxiety of waiting, separateness, or being with a narcissistic and self-preoccupied analyst who was not attending to him, or was trying to force her way into him. Later the hatred that drove his intrusions was more prominent – the degradation of the imagos he forced on and into me as being my identity, though he knew, if dimly, since he was not in a total state of projective identification, that these images were false perceptions.

Of course all this was interpreted piecemeal as it emerged. With time and analysis Mr B revealed unambiguously that the target of his hatred was knowing. He tilted himself backwards, stealthily bent his knees up, swayed his bottom over the couch, and consciously fantasised about undressing girls with his eyes, or feeling his 'breasts' on his chest, or awaiting a homosexual overture from a male friend known twenty years ago with whom he had never had sexual relations. He was perversely playing with troubling themes familiar to him from his analysis with contempt for an analyst who did not prohibit his excesses of erotised distortion on the couch. We began to realise that Mr B, in the mode Betty Joseph (1982) describes, was not so much playing as addicted to these phantasies. The realisation that he was enslaved to conscious fantasising that turned analytic thought into rubbish was very distressing to Mr B, but then his initially painful insight was turned into 'sexy slave phantasies' in which he was a slave forever rowing an ancient vessel, and, in due course, 'sexy slave phantasies' were continually intruding into his mind and plagued him.

The accessibility of such a cycle was part of a significant change taking place in Mr B. With the resolution of some of his anxieties, where previously he had split and dispersed some of the elements of his psychic life he was now tending to gather and assemble them. Mr B was more present and mentally active and some days I was astonished by his liveliness and capacity for thought. Some significant memories of family life returned. His earlier mental configuration in which to the fore were erotised dyads of soft girls, brute phalli, and bottoms, while in a recessive area were remote parents far apart with so little life or character they were almost spectral, was changing.

I come now to the period I present in detail. Mr B had left for the summer holiday in good spirits, notably freer from his usual anxieties and erotised preoccupations. In the new term he obtained a new contract which he told me about saying 'I got that job by the way. I explained to them I couldn't start early on some mornings'. His evident pleasure in his success, and his direct manner with me and with his new employers, were in good contrast to how he would previously have been very anxious about a clash of times between analysis and work, feel I was invading his career, try to exploit my guilt and act out to alienate his employers – once losing a prospective job in this way. There was a sense of separateness and difference.

Yet, along with his new directness the old destructive intrusive acting out continued. An ongoing example was a philosophy course he had begun that year. In several sessions just before those I report he came with his head full of books he was reading: Aristotle's *Ethics*, Boethius etc., etc. told in a way so that I wondered (as I often had) if he knew I had been a philosopher once, and/or that my husband was a philosopher still, teaching at the very university he was attending. I felt he knows, is watching me, 'reading me' from inside, and yet, of course, it could be a co-incidence. I felt invaded, and made impotent in analytic function. When I drew his attention to how he felt his eyes were inside me watching me not knowing what to do, he became again direct, and moreover was distressed by the inconstancy of the way he sees me.

MONDAY

Mr B started quickly, as though to pre-empt me coming in about my week-end, saying he had had a busy week-end. The chief event was that he had gone to a theatre to see a play with a group of people. After the theatre they had all gone to a restaurant. There were nine of them. It was late and he was hungry. The man who organised it, who should have ordered the main course right away, did not. Instead he ordered drinks. And after that, he ordered starters. It got very late so that by the time they left the restaurant it was after 1.30 AM.

During his lively telling, Mr B made me curious – I wondered: How does one find a restaurant in London these days that stays open so late? There had been pauses in Mr B's account, yet each time I wanted to come in, he said 'No', and talked on, giving me a taste of how it is to be a child refused entry to, and made curious about, night-time goings on, which eventually, when he let me, I interpreted. All so far had been straightforward.

Then Mr B repeated what he had said about the restaurant and the man who organised it and made the main course so late, going over it all, talking for a long time. I noticed how there were no names of the people, the theatre or the restaurant they had been to. There was a silence. Then Mr B said, 'There is something very annoying. I don't know what to do. Somebody is wanting a reference'. He stopped. I thought: Yes, I want a reference. I don't know what this is about or what is annoying. He broke the silence with more of the same about his week-end and then said, 'There was a review in a Sunday paper about . . .?' (he left his sentence incomplete). 'By Kathy . . .?' (he left the name incomplete). I did not complete his sentences or supply what most likely was the missing information – it so happened there had been an article that week-end in a Sunday paper in which some analysts, among them myself, were mentioned. Even this was tricky – it was an article not a review, and the writer's first name was not Kathy, though there has been a Kathy O'Shaughnessy writing reviews in Sunday papers, but not for a while now. Mr B waited, mentally inside my mind, I thought, watching to see how he had organised me. When I stayed quiet, he talked again about his week-end, sounding angry and isolated. His legs came up and he swayed his bottom in his usual way for a brief spell as he said he thought he might do some more philosophy even though there was no course he really liked and the group he'd organised had collapsed.

During these prevarications, which so evidently were prevarications, the atmosphere had quite changed. At the beginning of the session we had been straightforwardly engaged about issues of curiosity and exclusion on the week-end. Now, in place of curiosity there was an intrusive voyeurism aimed at preventing a continuation of a straightforward 'main course' to the session, although even as he persisted in trying to organise me into opening myself to his invasions he knew and was angry that he wasn't succeeding.

I eventually made a rather long interpretation. I hope it was of the kind Rosenfeld might call 'integrative'. I spoke about how he had let me see his two selves: one straightforward about the difficulty of feeling excluded and curious on the week-end, the other trying to organise us with a way of talking – telling, not telling, misleading – into seeming not separate but inside each other, watching in a knowing way. This self hates me to be potent with him and aims to delay and disable me so that I cannot continue to give him whatever should be the main course of the session that his other self is hungry for. I finished by saying he knows his attempted organising of us is failing, and he admits he doesn't even really like it, yet he is tempted to keep on doing it. There was a long silence. I added something. I said that I thought that when he'd been talking before he'd also recognised that it was the same disabling way in which for a long time in analysis he has been talking about philosophy. There was another long silence. Then Mr B responded in a straightforward and strong voice saying: 'I like what you said. Because it is accurate'.

As he left the session he turned and looked at me with respect.

TUESDAY

I was shutting the door of the consulting room as Mr B was going to the couch when he turned and took a few steps back to the door. He stood there, looking afraid and depressed, and said 'I need to get my handkerchief'. I opened the door for him, he went out, came back and lay down.

Making a broad gesture with his hand at the room, me and himself, he pronounced: 'There's no reality to any of this'. There was a long silence. When he spoke again his talk took him away, to a miscellany of things in his home and office. I said that I thought he felt trapped here and was now talking himself away and out, like before he had physically to get out of the room. Very hostile and negating, Mr B said 'No. I wanted my handkerchief. That's all,' crushing out meaning.

He began to talk about his handkerchief. 'What comes to mind is boarding school and masturbation. It's disgusting really' he said as he pulled out of his pocket an orange handkerchief with dots. He went on to say that when he goes to his old university town he buys these handkerchiefs from a special shop. One can also buy them in London in Jermyn Street, dotted like mine. Near the men's clubs, you know. My wife's first boy-friend has the same handkerchief! I often find it amusing he turned out to be homosexual. He's lived with his partner for thirty-five years. In fact they're the longest surviving couple among our friends. We all have the same handkerchiefs.

Mr B went on like this, trying to construct an exciting club atmosphere of masturbating men who hate women, along the way referring to and explicitly fouling some recent analytic work which had led to realisations of his own about his adolescence and couples and thirds. He ended talking to me as though he were chatting amusingly to a female companion at a dinner party. 'I've got two views about women: the public one – tolerant, feminist – of course they're equal! And also the old-fashioned one: a woman should revolve around the man – have his meal ready on the table, look after his clothes'. During all this he rubbed his forearm from time to time – everything short of actually masturbating his penis and ejaculating into his handkerchief had gone on. It felt excessive, a misuse of a session, as though a setting for analysis had been subverted into a room for sexual 'personal services' such as a brothel supplies. Even so, Mr B remained anxious and depressed, unable quite to sustain his belief in having me as a voyeur in a high world of homosexual males nor in his amusing me as a 'lady' companion, and I think it was disgusting to him to be driven to so destructive a masturbation phantasy.

I tried to make a link with the previous day's session, saying that yesterday he felt the self that intruded and disabled me felt caught and exposed, and now feared my hostility. I said I thought he was also frightened of his hatred, which feels so huge it's dotty, mad. I also pointed out how in yesterday's session he had hated me but also respected me, which makes him feel so bad he can't bear it, and so that he has to derealise it and make a phantasy world to get away into. I saw however that words – I was unable to find any interpretation that was of help – were unbearable and provoked further excesses. I stopped talking. I became a spectator, full with his evacuated depression and the acute pain of seeing my patient driven by fear, depression and hatred to enacting what he himself thinks is disgusting really.

WEDNESDAY

At first Mr B affected a thin cheeriness underneath which I could hear in him something so worn-down it was almost expiring. Then, snide and challenging, he gave a warped version of the previous session saying among other things that I had accused him of being a homosexual and a woman hater. I said I thought he wanted to provoke an argument to test whether I had enough life left in me to know a distorted version when I heard it. To this he replied 'Well. Yes.' and was briefly a little hopeful but then fell again into despair. I spoke about his despair that within himself he felt a world was almost dying after yesterday's session. He could not bear to hear me.

He got sleepy, struggled against it, succumbed. An atmosphere of ruin, hatred, despair was palpable.

He woke when I said it was time to stop. He left saying it was the worst session ever.

THURSDAY

In the waiting room Mr B looked lost. He lay low down on the couch in acute distress. He said he was cold. He said the central heating had broken down in his house all week and it had got very cold. (The weather in fact was very cold.) I said he was telling me he felt something central to do with warmth had broken down: he felt out in the cold, and within himself he also felt cold – he had no love left and he feared he was himself unloved.

He made some attempt to negate this painful psychic reality by means of unreal fantasising to raise a spark of warmth in himself or me. It was weak, confused and did not work; such constructions had been exposed as masturbation phantasies and had lost their power. Interpretations I tried were dead and useless.

Communication between us had broken down. At the end of the session which was the last of the week (he comes four times) Mr B left in acute distress.

It was now six weeks before the Christmas break. Mr B was gripped by wrenching anxieties. Both systems of central heating had broken down: enactment and erotisation on the one hand, and true warmth for and from his objects, on the other. He believed I did not like him because, as he put it, he had 'crossed a line', 'gone too far'. He feared his inner world was beyond repair, and felt trapped with fear, hatred and persecuting guilt towards his analyst.

He became doubtful about psychoanalysis. He said he knew when he came to me he needed something. He knew his life wasn't right. But was my method right for him? He presumed I thought it was, which was important to him. For several sessions he was tormented by doubts. Then he seized on the idea of escaping his torments by stopping analysis – after Christmas he would not return.

For a few days this plan relieved him, then he doubted it. He said feelingly 'I am tempted to stop and not return, but when I think of that I feel most unhappy', and he regained some inner freedom to think. He told me he recognised his present predicament and his impulse to give up analysis as a return of the terrible time he'd had a collapse at work, when his chief appointed someone who was his junior over him, and he gave up his job with a resulting hiatus in his career.

For a few sessions he was enormously relieved to be still with me and in analysis. A memory returned to him of standing on the edge of a steep valley in Jerusalem. Birds were flying in the fresh air, and he could see the dome of a church below. Mr B spoke so vividly he seemed there again, on his own, out in the fresh air, using his eyes not to intrude but to observe what's there. It could have been kitsch, or a setup for me. I did not think it was. I stayed quiet. Suddenly he produced some violating psychoanalese about this memory. His spoiling self had intruded and his liveliness vanished; he gave up and surrendered to sleepiness.

After this, his torments about what to do returned. There was an atmosphere of last chance and danger. I thought I might really lose my patient. Stopping analysis was multiply determined, but what was foremost was Mr B's fear of invasion by, and enslavement to, irreparably damaged objects. Typically, he was at this time reading a book about the abolition of slavery.

In the last fortnight Mr B made what he called a 'decision'. He would return after Christmas, but he would not come on Tuesdays. He was enormously relieved to have found a way to come back. He tried to force me to be overtly friendly about giving up Tuesdays, 'proving' to me that it made him feel better. He was again anxious, sleeping poorly, had diarrhoea, etc.

Not wanting to push him into a position which might make it impossible for him to return, I said nothing about what I would, or would not, do about his 'decision', except wondering out loud if he was unsure whether I was going to be able to stand up to him. He responded with sudden goodwill – 'Well, are you?'

He was still reading his book about slavery. He told me he always reads something while he eats his breakfast. He was 'reading me', excited that I was now 'enslaved' by his decision to return but not come on Tuesdays, but also anxious and guilty. In one of the last sessions he was more accessible and I spoke about his fear of his intrusive hatred that continues even while, so to say, he has his breakfast with me, and his fears that I will force into him a state of anxiety and guilt from which he will never escape and which will make it impossible for him ever to leave me, and how in this regard, not coming on Tuesdays, proves he can get out. To all of this he responded with a straightforward, appreciative 'Exactly right'. In one of his last sessions Mr B told me 'I'm still sticking to my decision about Tuesdays, though I know it's wrong'.

In his very last session he was rampant in a state of total phallic projectification, enacting equivalents of taking his trousers down and defecating on the couch and refusing to listen as I tried to speak about his being an image of an analyst shitting on him on this last day, an image he knew to be distorted to evade the pain of parting. Then, at the door as he left, he said pertly 'Have a good break', watching me, waiting to see me return his good wishes as I customarily do. This time I could not. I was suddenly too angry and just managed to say 'Good-bye'. Mr B had found my limits. He had provoked in me an anger that lasted for hours.

After Christmas Mr B returned, but not on Tuesdays.

DISCUSSION

In the Monday session after the week-end we see Mr B's two selves. One communicates in a straightforward way about going to a theatre and a restaurant, by projecting into me feelings of exclusion and curiosity such as a child might feel about night-life. Mr B's other self speaks in a different mode – half-telling, stimulating, misleading – with the aim of intruding into my mind and watching voyeuristically as he tries to delay and disable me from giving him what should be the main course of the session for which he is hungry. Mr B himself has seen what 'the man who organised it' is doing in the restaurant, and when I interpret how it is happening in the session Mr B likes it – as he says 'because it is accurate'.

At that moment Mr B has preferred an accurate analyst to his prevaricating self. In a way that is most disturbing for Mr B this upsets his more usual internal balance in which his prevaricating self, a narcissistic structure (I have left aside Mr B's narcissism – waiting to hear Dr Britton on the subject), feels superior, both to the analyst and his other self, both of whom it regards as his juniors. Indeed, later Mr B himself recognised that this analytic crisis was a repeat of a life crisis of some years before when a junior was appointed over him, making his place of work so intolerable that he gave up his job with a consequent hiatus in his career.

On the next day, Tuesday, his intrusive self, its idealised cover blown, feels trapped, frightened and depressed. He hates and fears the analyst who has become very threatening. Mr B tries to de-realise this situation, and with his dotted orange handkerchief to re-project himself into the identity of a popular misogynistic phallus in a world of split, inferior and seducible objects. However, he finds no sustainable power over me or himself and only reveals yet more clearly that these are aggressive masturbation phantasies whose purpose is to evade and destroy psychic reality. It was a horrible session. I could find no useful interpretation and was reduced to being a pained and depressed watcher of my patient.

On the next day, the one Mr B said 'was the worst session ever', he has internalised an analyst reduced to impotence. His despair about his hatred and the ruin of the analysis, which for him is concrete, overwhelms him and seeps out and envelops everything. By the end of the week Mr B's systems of central heating have broken down – both the excitement of intrusion and erotisation, and love for and from his objects. He is in an acute state of distress, tormented about what to do. Should he end his analysis? Or should he return after Christmas?

To give up his analysis was seen by Mr B as an escape from an analysis believed to be forcing into him unendurable pain and anxiety about himself and a damaged, irreparable world. Rosenfeld, in a discussion of this type of crisis (1964), draws attention to another feeling impelling the patient to give up at a time like this: unconsciously it is a self-sacrifice to appease the super-ego who, as Rosenfeld puts it, accuses the patient of building up his life at the analyst's expense. You will remember Mr B saying 'I knew when I came for a psychoanalysis that I needed something; I knew my life wasn't right'. I think Rosenfeld is right; stopping analysis would have meant to Mr B ending his hopes of a better life in order to appease his enormous sense of guilt.

Yet, to return after Christmas meant a return to a painful and uncertain prospect. He faced a struggle to renounce his orientation to and identification with his invasive self and to reorient himself to objects which arouse huge anxiety and distress. Any withdrawal from his substantial state of invasive projective identification painfully exposes his unmodified infantile self; terrified, greedy, envious, whose intolerance of real relations will continue to handicap him. Moreover, the way his objects have entered his mind means the analyst as a good figure on whom he can rely is peripheral, while more central is a persecuting analyst whom he fears will invade him with more than he can stand.

Can Mr B bear it? After all, he has his limits, and I have mine. It was difficult to discriminate when he was available for thinking from when he had projected himself all the way into his object and lost his capacity for verbal thought – which needed a different interpretive approach. At times I could not find any way to talk to him, especially when Mr B, in a state of projective identification with an omnipotent phallus, grossly enacted a masturbation phantasy.

Consider the last complex session, the one in which I was left full of anger. Mr B was intruding violently, venting his hatred of an analyst who takes a break from him and who persists in trying to understand him; he was misunderstanding the ending as his being forcibly ejected like shit, while refusing to listen to my saying that this might be his defence against parting, and misunderstanding too any quietness on the analyst's part as indifference – hence his excesses to penetrate. Mr B knows he 'goes too far', 'crosses a line', and I think he was trying to elicit the hatred of him he believes must be there inside me. This complex condensation of communication and evacuation, intrusion and distortion, plus his final provocation off the couch aroused an anger in me I could not hold.

In the event, as I reported, Mr B neither stopped nor returned fully. He came back, but not on Tuesdays. This made it possible for him to continue, yet it was also an acting out that attacked the framework of the analysis. Mr B was doing what Michael Feldman (1995) describes as 'a deal' with himself and with the analyst. In 1964 Rosenfeld warns the analyst to expect pressure from the patient for 'overtly friendly acting out' in such situations, and his view then was that the analyst should not act out with the patient in an 'overtly friendly' way but interpret the patient's underlying fear of the analyst as a persecuting figure. However, in his later book *Impasse and Interpretation* in the course of exploring factors in the patient and the analyst that either augment or resolve an impasse, his emphasis was different. He thought it better technique not to disturb the patient's idealisations too quickly – as is well-known, a controversial change of Rosenfeld's views. I have followed Rosenfeld's earlier understanding. I think Mr B is hungry for accuracy and something new from me, and it was important – while I accepted it to work with – not to collude with his deal, or prevaricate about his hostility, or his fear of me as a disturbing and invading figure. At that point it was still uncertain whether the crisis would become an impasse or whether my patient and I, in some way, would resolve it.

IN SUMMARY

After briefly describing prior stages of the analysis, the paper presents in detail the period when the analysis turned into a crisis. I am deeply indebted to Rosenfeld's understanding of the phenomenon of intrusive projective identification – so central in Mr B, and which I think always, even when less present in the personality, exerts a disproportionately large and pathological affect.

References

Feldman, M. (1995) 'Grievance', unpublished paper.

Freud, S. (1911) Formulation on the Two Principles of Mental Functioning, in *SE*, vol. 12, 215–26.

Joseph, B. (1982) 'Addiction to Near Death', in *International Journal of Psychoanalysis*, vol. 63, 449–56; reprinted in M. Feldman and E. Bott Spillius (eds), *Psychic Equilibrium and Psychic Change: Selected Papers of Betty Joseph* (1989), London: Routledge, 127–38.

Klein, M. (1946) 'Notes on Some Schizoid Mechanisms', in *International Journal of Psychoanalysis*, vol. 27, 99–110; reprinted in *The Writings of Melanie Klein* (1975), London: Hogarth Press, vol. 3, 1–24.

Klein, M. (1957) *Envy and Gratitude*, London: Tavistock; reprinted in *The Writings of Melanie Klein* (1975), London: Hogarth Press, vol. 3, 176–235.

Rosenfeld, H. (1952) 'Notes on the Psycho-Analysis of the Super-Ego Conflict of an Acute Schizophrenic Patient'. *International Journal of Psycho-Analysis*, 33, 111–31. Reprinted in *Psychotic States*, 63–103, London: Hogarth Press.

Rosenfeld, H. A. (1947) 'Analysis of a Schizophrenic State with Depersonalization', in *International Journal of Psychoanalysis*, vol. 28, 130–9; reprinted in *Psychotic States* (1965), London: Hogarth Press, 13–33.

Rosenfeld, H. A. (1964) 'An Investigation into the Need of Neurotic and Psychotic Patients to Act Out During Analysis', in *Psychotic States* (1965), London: Hogarth Press, 200–16.

Rosenfeld, H. A. (1987) *Impasse and Interpretation*. London: Tavistock.

Segal, H. (1991) *Dream, Phantasy, and Art*, London: Routledge.

Steiner, J. (1989) 'The Psychoanalytic Contribution of Herbert Rosenfeld', in *International Journal of Psychoanalysis*, vol. 70, 611–17.

Steiner, J. (1993) *Psychic Retreats: Pathological Organisations of the Personality in Psychotic, Neurotic, and Borderline Patients*, London: Routledge.

Chapter 2

Discussion of Edna O'Shaughnessy's paper

Michael Feldman

I should like to follow the way O'Shaughnessy orients us at the beginning of this fine, illuminating paper. She refers to the importance Rosenfeld attached to the patient's persecutory anxieties, the phantasy of the analyst forcing himself into the patient in order to control and rob. Rosenfeld understood these phantasies as derived from the patient's projection of parts of his own personality, particularly those that embodied primitive impulses to invade, to possess and control, into the analyst who becomes identified, in the patient's mind, with these projected parts. The patient feels driven to defend himself against such an invasive and destructive object by a variety of mechanisms, such as withdrawal, avoidance, and the negating of interpretations.

O'Shaughnessy describes very vividly the way her patient needed to intrude in an omnipotent fashion into her – into her body and her mind. He become partially identified with a girl with breasts, or a person in possession of pieces of the analyst's knowledge. He could create and sustain confusion within his own mind and attempt to invade the analyst with excited and erotised confusion about her identify and her functions. It seemed that these identifications were attempts to defend himself against any clear awareness of separateness, to fulfil his greed, and to diminish his feelings of envy, although they also created problems for him, such as anxieties of entrapment, and a sense of the loss of self.

The aspects of this paper I would like to focus on, however, are the consequences for this patient of the projection of these elements of himself into the analyst, and the persecutory anxieties that inevitably follow, which O'Shaughnessy outlined at the start of her paper. Although the patient refers to his objects being indifferent, cold, or dead and forgotten, I wondered about the extent to which he actually felt dominated by a primitive terror of being invaded, controlled and destroyed by an object driven by hatred and greed.

O'Shaughnessy refers to the emergence of the fact that the target of Mr B's hatred was knowing. I thought he felt threatened by knowledge of the nature and extent of his fears of his objects, and it was this knowledge in particular that had to be attacked. Instead of allowing himself to know about his fears of the object intruding and attacking him through his anus, for example, he played out a provocative and perverse mockery of this on the couch, referred to a homosexual overture from twenty years ago, or turned his fears into 'sexy slave phantasies'.

And yet, O'Shaughnessy describes how, as a result of her work with him, there was a move towards integration, and she gives an example of how he could be more lively, more direct and appreciative after a holiday, when he had obtained a new job. However, he seemed able to tolerate the sense of separateness and difference only for a short time, and O'Shaughnessy then refers to his need once again to invade her life, her family and her interests, in his mind.

In the Monday session, which O'Shaughnessy describes in greater detail, although the patient begins talking in a lively and clear way, describing an experience of delay and frustration in the week-end restaurant, we are shown very beautifully how the patient's experience of separation and exclusion is re-created in the session, but now it is the analyst who is confronted with pauses, hesitations, frustration and curiosity. The patient says, after a while, 'There is something very annoying. I don't know what to do. Somebody is wanting a reference'. He continued to speak in a tricky, intrusive and pro-vocative fashion, and the analyst observes 'and then his bottom swayed in the usual way'. I have the impression that, in this context, 'Somebody is wanting a reference' represents the disavowed needs and desires which have been projected. However, the object is not possessed of an ordinary desire for information or knowledge to help her orientate herself, but the nature of the patient's desires which have been projected make her into a fearful 'somebody' which he has to defend himself against, and which increases his sense of isolation.

However, after some time and no doubt a good deal of internal work, O'Shaughnessy was able to make what I believe Rosenfeld would indeed have admired as an 'integrative' interpretation, to which the patient res-ponded in a straightforward and strong voice, acknowledging, with respect, the accuracy of her interpretation. I want to come back to this part of the material, but this session was followed by one in which the patient seemed to feel trapped, and behaved once more in a hostile, perverse and negating fashion. This led O'Shaughnessy to interpret that after the previous session he felt caught and exposed, and now feared she was hostile to him, as well as being frightened of his own hatred.

In his 1971 paper, Rosenfeld pointed out that when the psychotic patient, living in a state of projective identification with the analyst, begins to experience himself as a separate person, violent destructive impulses make their appearance.

> His aggressive impulses are sometimes an expression of anger related to separation anxiety, but generally they have a distinctly envious

character. As long as the patient regards the analyst's mind and body and his help and understanding as part of his own self he is able to attribute everything that is experienced as valuable in the analysis as being part of his own self . . . As soon as a patient begins to feel separate from the analyst the aggressive reaction appears and particularly clearly so after a valuable interpretation, which shows the analyst's understanding. The patient reacts with feelings of humiliation, complains that he is made to feel small; why should the analyst be able to remind him of something which he needs but which he cannot provide for himself. In his envious anger the patient tries to destroy and spoil the analyst's interpretations by ridiculing or making them meaningless. The analyst may have the distinct experience in his counter transference that he is meant to feel that he is no good and has nothing of value to give to the patient.

(Rosenfeld 1971: 123 and p. 137 this volume)

I suspect with this patient, the experience of the analyst as a thoughtful, separate object, that he can respect and value for a while gives rise to a massive projective identification, with the consequent paranoid anxieties which O'Shaughnessy referred to at the beginning of her paper. Thus, as O'Shaughnessy describes, following the brief experience of more direct contact with a separate object he could value, Mr B seemed to withdraw into a bleak, cold and lonely world, full of despair, in which there was no love, only fear and persecution. After a struggle he seemed to arrive at a compromise solution – a partial withdrawal. I thought he articulated his terrible fears that the analyst would so invade and possess him that he would indeed be a helpless and lost slave to her, with no mind, and no body of his own, and it was striking that when O'Shaughnessy interpreted this to him, he confirmed the interpretation in a clear and direct way. However, I suspect that once again, the very fact that he felt he had been seen and understood by the analyst as a separate and thoughtful person gave rise to the same pressure to retreat into provocative, perverse masturbatory activity where he felt more in control.

I think O'Shaughnessy has shown us very convincingly this ill and vulnerable man's need to use projective identification to defend himself against unbearable experiences of separation and envy. She also illustrates the way the defensive movements have become recruited into the type of perverse organisation described by Rosenfeld, and further elaborated by Steiner (1993) with the erotised excitement and gratification this provides for the patient.

Rosenfeld (1971) has described situations in which the patient uses projective identification primarily for the denial of psychic reality.

In this situation the patient splits off parts of his self in addition to impulses and anxieties and projects them into the analyst for the purpose of evacuating and emptying out the disturbing mental content which leads to a denial of psychic reality. As this type of patient primarily wants the analyst to condone the evacuation process and the denial of his problems, he often reacts to interpretations with violent resentment, as they are experienced as critical and frightening since the patient believes that unwanted unbearable and meaningless mental content is pushed back into him by the analyst.

(1971: 121 and p. 135 this volume)

When the patient's mind is so dominated the analyst may not be able to find any way of interpreting to the patient which does not provoke such responses, and Britton (1989: 88–9) has given a vivid clinical example of just such a predicament.

Exploring these situations further, Rosenfeld argued that 'omnipotent projective identification interferes with the capacity of verbal and abstract thinking and produces a concreteness of the mental processes which leads to confusion between reality and phantasy'. The patient who is using excessive projective identification 'is dominated by concrete thought processes which cause misunderstanding of verbal interpretations, since words and their content are experienced by the patient as concrete, non-symbolic objects' (op. cit., p. 122).

What then enabled O'Shaughnessy's patient at certain moments to hear and understand her interpretations as interpretations, and not assaults, reflecting her thoughtfulness and care, to which he could respond in a direct and appreciative way? O'Shaughnessy does provide us with some clues. She says, 'I think Mr B is hungry for accuracy and it was important not to prevaricate about his hostility and fear of me as a persecuting and invading figure'. In other words, there was an aspect of the patient that was interested in communicating, and in being understood in a direct, and non-perverse fashion, which it was extremely important to recognise. However, the mobilisation and the constructive use of this capacity in the patient depends in a crucial way on the analyst's mode of functioning.

In another paper, Rosenfeld pointed out that

> The analyst's capacity to perceive and tolerate the non-verbal projections of the patient is often clearly shown in the way he gives his interpretation because only if he can inwardly tolerate and remain in lively contact with the projected material will the communication with the patient remain meaningful and alive.

(1972: 459)

He quotes a very disturbed patient saying, after some years of analysis,

> I cannot look and see what is there by myself, but when you take the trouble to inspect it carefully and tell me what you see, then I can begin

to look at it myself and I begin to exist. When you do not put things clearly into words, I feel you do not understand and I get afraid you have given up with me or can't bear me and I feel dead and empty.

(ibid.)

Rosenfeld felt it was enormously important for the analyst to recognise and to acknowledge the patient's need and desire for direct communication and understanding, and that the analyst should recognise the presence of a healthier, non-perverse aspect of the personality, however much this was attacked and tyrannised by something destructive in the patient. This is one reason why he attached a good deal of importance to the process of describing to the patient in great detail what he understood what was going on within the patient, and in the transference, conveying a marvellous sense of balance, which reflected his deep understanding and sympathy for different aspects of the patient.

To give one brief example, he describes part of his work with a psychotic patient as follows:

I interpreted to him that after he felt that he was making progress and feeling separate from me he was suddenly overcome with impatience and envy of me and other men who were able to move about and were active. I suggested that it was the envious part which drove him into the identification with other men and myself in order to take over their strength and potency, and in this way the omnipotent part of himself could make him believe that he could be mature and healthy instantly. He agreed with the interpretation without any difficulty and started to speak very fast: he said he knew all this and was quite aware of it, but he also knew that this belief was quite false and that it was a delusion and he was angry at having to listen to a voice in him which was very persuasive and stimulated him to take over the mind and body of other people.

(1971: 130 and pp. 142–3 this volume)

Let us go back to the Monday session which O'Shaughnessy has described, where the patient spoke about the visit to the restaurant over the week-end. The relatively lively communication which raised issues of curiosity and exclusion evoked in turn a more perverse acting out, provocation, intrusion, prevarication. However, it seems important that O'Shaughnessy was able to maintain her balance, and to go on observing and thinking about the patient. As she says, '. . . even as he persisted in trying to organise me into opening myself to his invasions he knew and was angry that he wasn't succeeding'. She then made a relatively long and complex interpretation, which addressed two aspects of the patient, the relationship of each to what the analyst was offering.

I think there are two important, related elements at work here. First the fact that, after a good deal of thought, the analyst put clearly into words what she saw happening in the patient in the course of the session. Her capacity to do so in a balanced way, which conveyed to the patient that she was not especially disturbed by the hostility, excitement or despair he might have evoked, reassured the patient about her state of mind, and her relationship to him. The temporary and partial protection from anxiety and guilt about the physical and mental state of his object allowed his paranoid anxieties to diminish.

However, the very fact of the analyst's separateness, the demonstration of her capacity to function in a three-dimensional way, engaged in an intercourse with her own internal objects, without being too controlled or disrupted by the patient provokes his jealousy, envy and hatred. This led to the renewal of his efforts to invade and disturb her mind and body, with the consequent inevitable upsurge in paranoid anxieties about her violent intrusive retaliation.

Returning to the start of O'Shaughnessy's paper, Rosenfeld has drawn our attention to the importance of the disturbed patient's persecutory anxieties about an invading analyst, which can so interfere with the analyst's interpretive efforts. Much of his subsequent writing has been devoted to trying to describe ways in which the analyst can function that make it possible for the patient to hear him and make use of him in a constructive fashion. He stressed the importance of offering the patient detailed, and balanced interpretations of the functions and relationship between different parts of their personality, and with the analyst. Edna O'Shaughnessy's paper describes the way in which the analyst is disturbed by the patient's projections, but is then able to recover her balance and capacity for thought. When, as a consequence, she offers him an impressive integrative interpretation he is able to respond in a direct and constructive way, before becoming once again possessed by the need to defend himself against experiences of separation and envy by not only attacking the analyst and her work, but also his own capacities for knowledge and understanding.

References

Britton, R. (1989) 'The Missing Link', in J. Steiner (ed.), *The Oedipus Complex Today*, London: Karnac, 83–101.

Rosenfeld, H. (1971) 'Contributions to the Psychopathology of Psychotic Patients: The Importance of Projective Identification in the Ego Structure and Object Relations of the Psychotic Patient', in P. Doucet and C. Laurin (eds), *Problems of Psychosis*, Amsterdam: Excerpta Medica; reprinted in E. Bott Spillius, *Melanie Klein Today. 1. Mainly Theory* (1988), London: Routledge.

Rosenfeld, H. (1972) 'A Critical Appreciation of James Strachey's Paper on the Nature of the Therapeutic Action of Psychoanalysis', in *International Journal of Psychoanalysis*, vol. 53, 455–61.
Steiner, J. (1993) *Psychic Retreats*, London: Routledge.

Chapter 3

What part does narcissism play in narcissistic disorders?

Ronald Britton

No one contributed more to the psychoanalytic understanding of narcissism and narcissistic disorders in the second half of the twentieth century than Herbert Rosenfeld. His brilliant clinical accounts have influenced many, and his ideas about the nature of narcissistic disorders have been incorporated into the thinking of many psychoanalysts.

In 1964 he suggested that Freud's notion of "primary narcissism" could best be regarded as a primitive object relation; he described the use of projective identification to create a narcissistic type of object relationship with others and he described the development of "narcissistic organisations" within the personality. In his 1971 paper on "the aggressive aspects of narcissism" he formulated his concept of "destructive narcissism" – a force derived from or exemplifying the death instinct. I would like to highlight some of his ideas for the purposes of this chapter.

1   Rosenfeld thought narcissistic disorders originated when there was a failure of primary splitting between good and bad in the paranoid–schizoid position. The risk of this was enhanced by lack of containment (Bion) or holding (Winnicott).

2   The narcissistic patient built up a phantasy of an omnipotent self and an omnipotently created object, often personified as a good friend or guru. The analyst, unless he colludes with this, is perceived as a threat to this relationship.

3   Later he added, "Hidden in the omnipotent [narcissistic] structure is an envious, destructive super-ego" (Rosenfeld 1987: 88–9). Bion earlier had described the production of an "ego destructive super-ego" as a consequence of a failure of containment in infancy (Bion 1959: 107). More recently Edna O'Shaughnessy (1999), and I (Britton 2003) have written at greater length on the concept of an ego-destructive super-ego and Leslie Sohn in a recent, as yet unpublished, paper emphasised the importance of this in some murderous individuals.

4   In 1987 Rosenfeld wrote that he now realised the need to distinguish between narcissistic organisations and a hidden deadly force that may

lie behind some of them. This force he characterised as manifested by murderous intent and idealisation of death. He described an analysis where it took the form of obsessive preoccupation with plans to murder the analyst (1987: 133).

5   Rosenfeld thought it important to distinguish between those narcissistic states in which the libidinal aspects predominate, from those where the destructive aspects of narcissism predominate.

Though he produced these general ideas he was always concerned primarily with individual cases and he left us with some tasks he regarded as clinically imperative. One was the need to distinguish between the operation of libidinal and destructive narcissism; another was the need to uncover the part played by trauma in cases of narcissistic disorder. His work leaves us pondering some questions that I will try to address in this paper. What do we mean by narcissism? Is there a difference between libidinal and destructive narcissism? What part does narcissism play in the narcissistic disorders?

WHAT DO WE MEAN BY NARCISSISM?

There is probably no area of psychoanalytic literature more profuse and muddling than that on narcissism. As well as there being different developmental models that complicate any discussion of narcissism, the confusion is further compounded because the word is used in different senses. So before considering anything else I would like to clarify my uses of the term.

As I see it, the term narcissism is used in the literature in three ways. First, to denote the phenomenon of clinical narcissism, in which there is a turning from interest in external objects to self-preoccupation. Second, the word is used to refer to a specific group of personality dysfunctional cases called the narcissistic disorders. And, third, the word narcissism is used to describe a force within the personality that opposes relationships to any objects other than the self. I would describe this as a destructive instinct opposed to relationships with any distinctly separate object; I call it a xenocidal instinct, many colleagues subsume it under the title "death instinct".

Clinical narcissism features in major psychiatric syndromes, minor disorders, and everyday life. In this chapter I want to put that aside and concentrate on the inner force we call narcissism and on the clinical states we call narcissistic personality disorder, in order to discuss the question what part does narcissism play in narcissistic disorders?

Henri Rey described these syndromes as, "a certain kind of personality disorder which defied classification into the two great divisions of neurosis and psychosis. We now know them as borderline, narcissistic, or schizoid personality organisation" (1979: 484). What sufferers of these various syndromes have in common is that they cannot, at least initially, function in analysis in an ordinary way because they cannot form an ordinary trans-ference relationship. Some remain aloof and detached, others are adherent, clamorous and concrete in their transference attachment but in neither situation is the analyst experienced as both significant and separate.

In order to discuss these questions further I will first briefly review the history of the concept.

THE DEVELOPMENT OF THE CONCEPT OF NARCISSISM

The germs of the distinction between libidinal and destructive narcissism can be found in the history of the development of the concept. From its beginning two themes have run in contrapuntal fashion through the dis-course on clinical narcissism. One theme is of narcissism as a defence against adverse object relations; the other theme is of narcissism as a manifestation of basic hostility to object relations. Even the original myth of Narcissus exists in two versions: one solipsistic, the other traumatic. Ovid's familiar account has Narcissus paying a price for his rejection of all other than himself, but Pausanius collected another version in which Narcissus lost a twin-sister and mistook his reflection for his lost twin (Radice 1973).

One could make a useful, though imprecise generalisation, that Freud's thinking leads us to the concept of libidinal narcissism whilst Abraham's ideas lead us to the notion of destructive narcissism. Freud made clear he saw secondary narcissism as a means of preserving or restoring love when object love appeared impossible, whilst Abraham's emphasis was on the hostility to transference objects that could be found in narcissistic disorders. Freud described self-love as substituting for mother love in narcissistic characters whilst Abraham described envy as promoting narcissism and retarding object love.

From the beginning Abraham linked it to "negativism": "The negativism of dementia praecox is the most complete antithesis to transference", he wrote in the first psychoanalytic paper to address the subject (1908: 71). Initially Abraham made this suggestion in a letter to Freud, whom he had yet to meet. Abraham proposed that, in contrast to hysteria, "dementia praecox destroys the person's capacity for sexual transference, i.e. for object love" (ibid.: 69). Abraham's notion was that the individual with this dis-order turned from all love objects, reverting instead to auto-erotism. Freud was clearly impressed and convinced that Abraham's theory was right.

The term narcissism was taken and developed by Freud from Paul Nacke and Havelock Ellis (Freud 1914), who described the attitude of someone who treated his body as a sexual object. Freud's own original contributions to narcissism began in a footnote that he added in 1910 to his "Three

Essays on the Theory of Sexuality" in which he described narcissistic object relations. Theorising about male homosexuals Freud wrote:

> in the earliest years of their childhood, [they] pass through a short lived but very intense fixation to a woman (usually their mother). And that, after leaving this behind, they identify themselves with a woman and take themselves as their sexual object. That is to say, they proceed from a narcissistic basis and look for a young man who resembles themselves and whom they may love as their mother loved them.
>
> (1905, footnote: 144–5)

In his 1914 paper "On Narcissism" Freud takes further his thinking on this wish for the ideal of mother–infant love. Ordinarily, falling in love, as he sees it, depletes the self in favour of the object whose reciprocal love is the only means of remedying this haemorrhage of libido. Those unfortunate enough to find love unrequited are thus deprived of self-esteem as well as the other's love. Secondary narcissism, however, according to Freud only occurs when there is some obstacle to the fulfilment of object love for internal reasons. He wrote:

> the satisfaction of love is impossible, and the re-enrichment of the ego can be supplied only by a withdrawal of libido from its objects. The return of the object libido to the ego and its transformation into narcissism represents, as it were, a happy love once more; and, on the other hand, it is also true that a real happy love corresponds to the primal condition in which object libido and ego libido cannot be distinguished.
>
> (1914: 99–100)

Suddenly in this last sentence we are presented by Freud with the notion that the fully fledged libidinal narcissist is in love with himself in just such a way as someone else might be "in love" with another person. But is it really another person if "happy love corresponds to the primal condition in which object libido and ego libido cannot be distinguished"? In this passage Freud implies that this "primal" – "happy love" – is essentially narcissistic object love, whether pursued with another person in the external world or as a love affair with the self in the internal world. In both situations, whether it is with an external or an internal object, the positive relationship is conditional on the elimination of difference.

If this is the case then a "narcissistic state" is not simply withdrawal from external objects to an internal object but to a particular kind of object relationship. This seems to me like a description of an ideal relationship between self and ego that has displaced the relationship between ego and super-ego: twin internal souls united by a narcissistic love that makes redundant the ego's need for the love from the super-ego that Freud thought a necessary condition for living. Is a narcissistic state an evasion of the super-ego? Are narcissistic object relations an alternative to loving the super-ego? If this were so might it be prompted by fear of a hostile super-ego, or an unreceptive super-ego or by envy of a powerful, unimpeachable, super-ego? I think I have met all of these possibilities clinically.

On the other hand if we follow Abraham's thinking on narcissism we find ourselves following a theme that culminated in Rosenfeld's concept of destructive narcissism. In his 1908 paper Abraham linked the withdrawal from object love to auto-erotism in patients with dementia praecox to their negativism. In his next major contribution to the subject he suggested that the excessive self-regard of some patients was linked to contempt and hostility towards their love-objects. In his paper on "Ejaculatio Praecox" (1917), he described narcissism as a source of sexual resistance. "[T]heir object love is very imperfect. Their true love-object is themselves. In accordance with Freud's view, we find . . . a particularly high and abnormally emotional estimation of the penis". Abraham went further and coupled this self-love with hostile contempt for women: "[H]e takes revenge on every woman for the disappointments of love to which as a child his mother subjected him" (ibid.: 297).

In his work on "the psychogenesis of melancholia", he described clinical narcissism as existing in both a positive and negative form: positive when it is manifest as self-admiration, and negative when it manifest itself as self-denigration (1924).

Two years after his description of phallic narcissism he wrote the first paper that properly described narcissistic disorder as a psychoanalytic entity, "A Particular Form of Neurotic Resistance against the Psycho-Analytic Method" (1919). In this he described a small group of patients who could not comply with the psychoanalytic method though appearing to do so, and commented that "it was those among my patients who had the most pronounced narcissism" (304–5).

This paper of Abraham was the starting point for Rosenfeld's first major paper on narcissistic disorders in 1964. It also influenced two important papers published in 1936 that linked Abraham's description of narcissistic character disorder with the negative therapeutic reaction. One was by Joan Riviere and the other by Karen Horney. Riviere's paper (1936) brought to the previous understanding of negative reactions in analysis Klein's new theory of the depressive position and the manic defence, and added her own concept of "defensive organisations". Horney (1936) emphasised the patient's compulsive rivalry with the analyst and also their demand for unconditional love. They need affection to reassure themselves against a double anxiety – anxiety concerning awareness and expression of their own hostility, and anxiety concerning retaliation from without.

Rosenfeld took further Horney's description of the patient's reaction to the analyst's work and Riviere's concept of defensive organisations. He elaborated his own theory of the "narcissistic organisation" within the personality that was opposed to real object relations and enlisted the allegiance of the patient by seduction, control and tyranny.

Rosenfeld thought it important to distinguish between those narcissistic states in which the libidinal aspects predominate from those where the destructive aspects of narcissism predominate. In the first, though envy, resentment and revenge erupt when the narcissistic belief system is punctured, this enhances understanding and diminishes the negativism. By contrast in the second, predominantly destructive narcissism, the envy is more violent and unacknowledged and there is an overwhelming wish to destroy the analyst or the self. In these cases he commented "death is idealised as a solution to all problems" (1987: 106–7).

Hanna Segal describes herself as differing from Rosenfeld on the question of the differentiation of destructive and libidinal narcissism. For her there is only destructive narcissism. However, she does this by confining the term to that force within narcissistic organisations that is fundamentally hostile to object relationships. "In narcissism, life-giving relationships and healthy self-love are equally attacked" (1997: 84), she wrote, "envy and narcissism are like two sides of a coin" (1997: 78). Love of the self and by implication Freud's description of the "happy love" of narcissistic relationships she subsumes under the life instincts which she sees as basically object loving and not narcissistic. Inasmuch as she is referring to narcissism as a force within the personality I am in complete agreement with her. But unlike Hanna Segal I use the term narcissistic disorders and include within them a range of phenomena, some destructive, some libidinal and some defensive. So when considering these I agree with Rosenfeld and attempt to distinguish between those predominantly destructive and those predominantly libidinal, though I prefer to call the latter predominantly defensive.

John Steiner (1987) subsumed these under his wider term "pathological organisations", which he sees as combining defences with destructive and libidinal narcissistic forces. His awareness that there is an inevitable mixture of motives driving these narcissistic systems leads him to oppose classification (personal communication 1999). Nevertheless, in my opinion, whatever the mixture and however much it might vary, the principal motive at any one time is either libidinal/defensive, or hostile/destructive. The formation of a narcissistic object relationship can be motivated by the wish to preserve the capacity for love by making the love-object seem like the self; or it can be aimed at annihilating the separate object. Aggression may result from either predominantly defensive or predominantly destructive narcissism. But there is a difference between fighting to retain love and the wanton violence of object hostility. In the social realm war can be defensive, and patriotic aggression can be misguided love, but genocide is neither: it is prompted by the wish to annihilate the other.

I will briefly describe two patients in order to illustrate how I see this distinction. The first I would describe as suffering from a predominantly destructive narcissistic disorder and the second from a predominantly defensive narcissistic disorder.

What they have in common is the production, by projective identification, of a narcissistic relationship with an ego ideal in order to evade a relationship with a destructive, parental super-ego. In the first case however the destructiveness is carried over into the twin-relationship, this then becomes a murderous alliance, whereas in the second case it becomes a psychic retreat where primal "happy love" is sought in mutual understanding.

CASE MATERIAL

Twin self vs. old woman

I would like to give a brief example from the supervision of a narcissistic patient. Dr A., the analyst, particularly wanted this supervision because though the analysis had just started she already felt in considerable difficulty. Dr A., a conscientious, skilful analyst with experience of analysing disturbed and difficult patients, could not understand her inability to establish and maintain an analytic setting with this patient.

She described a series of uncharacteristic lapses that resulted in her making concessions to her patient which she had not intended and which she immediately regretted. It made her feel the analysis was out of her control.

The patient Ms B., a pretty young woman, consulted the analyst when she became upset by the end of a relationship with a man. She also had a history of adolescent disturbance and episodes of anorexia. She was leaving the city where she had lived with the man to return to the city where her rich father lived with his second wife and where she would have analysis. All was arranged but when the removal men turned up on the day of her departure she sent them away and missed the plane.

Having arrived in her new home and arranged the beginning of her analysis she missed the first session. She rang to explain that she had lost the number of the consulting room. Dr A., sensing the need to establish her analytic stance and method of work from the outset, "firmly resolved" to discuss the question of payment for the missed session. It was the inexplicable loss of this "firm resolve" and others that alarmed the analyst. In the event Ms B. who was supposed to give the cheque at the end of the month failed to do so and Dr A. to her chagrin failed to draw attention to this. Following this session the patient, who by any standards was very wealthy, rang Dr A. to say she could not continue the analysis as she could not afford it. Dr A. suggested that she should come at the time of her next session and they could discuss it. The patient agreed to this and then Dr A., to her consternation despite her firm resolve not to talk on the phone, found herself involved in a fruitless further exchange with the patient. The patient then came to the next session twenty minutes early causing some disruption in the process.

In this session Ms B. lay on the couch rumpling it with her restless movements and several times left it to get sweets or tissues. What most troubled the analyst however was her own behaviour. In that session she amazed herself by agreeing to reduce the patient's fee. Her feeling that her counter-transference was out of control was further increased when, despite having addressed this problem before the next session in self-examination, she then unwittingly went overtime with the patient, something she rarely did. It was in this session, however, that a dream the patient recounted threw some light on these events.

> "I had this weirdest dream", said L, "I was in this house – this weird house – every dream season I have recurring dreams about a new house. This one is new – but I remember by sensory experience coming back to it from a hundred years ago. I am with another person who was my lover – or sister – or sibling, not sure what sex. I was neither male not female – neither or both. I was protecting the other one – we lived with an old lady – we plotted to kill her. This involved staircases and something written, like a letter, apparently giving her the letter without her seeing us do so would result in her death. We needed to do that for ourselves. But six or seven years later we got busted. I know it was me in the dream – I usually don't lie – [she lies all the time added the analyst] I remember thinking this is the first time – they won't find me out. They won't find out we are executing the murder. If she, the old woman, knew she would retaliate. She was like a malicious old woman – an evil force. It was murdering not from malice but life or death for me. The reason was this internal struggle. I had this taste in my mouth like a huge wad of gum – it was cannibalism – like chewing tasteless meat."
>
> The patient continued, "I was nauseous this morning when I awoke, eventually I vomited".

There is no doubt a great deal condensed in this dream. The patient herself identified the malicious old woman with her mother. I thought, in supervision, that the dream could best be used to account for what was actually taking place in the analysis and what light it might throw on the problem of repeated enactments.

I suggested that if we took Dr A. to be represented in the dream as both the "twin soul" conspirator and also as the malicious old woman the recent events would make sense. Dr A.'s unconscious counter-transference identification with her patient was represented in the dream as the patient's "twin soul". The plot by the twin souls to kill the "malicious old lady" could then be seen as an unconscious collusion between patient and analyst to kill off Dr A.'s professional self. Several small murders had already taken place, all of which were justified in the minds of the twin souls because they believe they are in danger of being fed poisonous cannibal meat by the weird practices of psychoanalysis.

The analyst regained her usual analytic stance, only to lose it again from time to time when her patient would dramatically introduce some unexpected complication into the analysis. A pattern emerged of forward movement followed by negative therapeutic reactions.

As the analysis progressed the full extent of the patient's disturbance became clearer. She had a drug problem and her episodic bulimia and vomiting was of long standing. Her bisexuality was evident both from the unfolding history and from the transference. In particular there were periods of oscillation between a homosexual erotic transference and a negative, paranoid, transference.

What I want to emphasise is my notion that the narcissistic object relations developed by this patient, the "twin soul" relationship, is an alliance formed to oppose a murderous super-ego, represented by the "old woman". However, the destructiveness is carried over into the narcissistic relationship. The purpose of the libidinal bond, expressed in the erotic transference, was to create an alliance whose aim was murder.

A dream from eighteen months later in the analysis threw further light on this complex narcissistic organisation.

> Dream. The patient, Ms B., is feeding a baby with a spoon – her mother is in the room – Ms B. is unsure whose baby it is. As she feeds, the spoon becomes a fork and the fork takes off the skin from the baby's lips who then eats it. She turns to her mother for help. Her mother says you do it like this: she takes off bigger chunks of the baby's mouth with the fork and says this is what the baby eats.
>
> The patient, Ms B., says there must be another way, so that the baby doesn't have to eat itself. The baby's lips are very red and firmly shut and look like genitals.
>
> Then she realises it isn't her mother it is X, a former girl friend and that they are not feeding a baby but having sex.
>
> "In real life" said the patient, she had a homosexual sexual relationship with X. "X", she said, "had the ideal body – I adored it – what I mean by ideal is that she had just the body I imagined my father would have wanted a woman to have".
>
> "We were together at College", she added. "It reminds me I used to have a recurrent masturbatory phantasy at that time – in it I was watching a man with steel toed boots kicking a woman in the genitals until the clitoris fell off".

There are many aspects to this analysis and the dream. For my present purpose I want to focus on the patient's sexual relationship with her own ego-ideal, represented by X, who usurped the mother's place in the primal scene. An idyllic, illusional, narcissistically based homosexual primal scene then displaced the horrific scene between mother and child. However, the persecutory phantasies follow the defensive movement and take the horrors of the infant-feeding phantasy into the primal scene where they become the basis of a consciously entertained perverse, sadistic phantasy.

PREDOMINANTLY LIBIDINAL OR DEFENSIVE NARCISSISM

The second case, Mrs D., was a woman who was head of a successful academic department. She came seeking analysis a year after having terminated by mutual agreement a lengthy psychotherapy; at the time of that ending she felt in good shape. She came now because she was afraid of "breaking down" completely, "whatever that means", she said. She described being in continuous distress and obsessed by a relationship with a young man; this was not sexual but had been intellectually intimate. She thought her feelings were completely irrational and told me it had happened before with another young man in the early days of her previous treatment. Both young men were junior colleagues in the academic department of which she was the head. Both relationships followed the same pattern. Initially she felt they understood each other completely and were of one mind. Later she became distressed when this mutual understanding could not be sustained.

She regarded herself as happily married and her children were central to her life but once established the relationship with the young men in her mind absorbed her attention completely. Fears that they would cease to value her and what she had given them haunted her. When anything took place that gave substance to this idea she believed herself to be a bad and worthless person. The love, admiration, respect and approval of her husband, children and friends though it gave comfort in no way mitigated the power of the young men's attitude over her self-regard.

The configuration underlying the obsessive relationship with the young men became clearer. She was an only child of separated parents. Her mother suffered from a severe narcissistic disorder and her father's self-centredness and vanity was legendary. In the course of analysis she was taken aback by having dreams which included a brother. In the dreams she was not surprised by the brother's presence. The figure was not anyone she had ever seen but she knew he was her brother. She had an imaginary companion throughout childhood and added that she had in adolescence an intimate but platonic friendship with a young man.

The intense emotional dependence on the young men's appreciation was in contrast to her relationship with those on whom she really depended, such as her husband. This relationship though warm was protected from her expectations particularly of understanding and hence from disappointment and dissatisfaction. Her transference to me followed this pattern. Though she clearly benefited when understood she did not seek it, but neither did she resist it, she simply avoided expecting it. The analytic transference like her marital relationship followed the pattern of that with her parents; it was to be preserved by her strictly limiting her expectations of it, and seeking a soul mate elsewhere. She believed that to turn for understanding to a parental object would lead to complete disappointment and risk a degree of mis-understanding that would negate her own subjective existence.

This twin soul-mate had an additional aspect to that of being her ideal-self. This ideal young man was always believed, by her, to be the primary love-object of an ideal mother such as she had never known. In the twin-relationship she was able therefore to play both parts, playing the ideal mother and by projective identification experiencing vicariously the love she had never received.

Both patients I see as having an ego-destructive super-ego, but with a difference. In Ms B., the first patient, the super-ego figure is a murderous woman; in Mrs D. the place usually occupied by an internal mother appears to be a void; not simply an absence but a negating presence. The rela-tionship with the super-ego is evaded in both cases by forming an attach-ment with the ego-ideal forming a narcissistic organisation. This is realised externally in a relationship with an idealised twin. In the first patient this becomes a perverse, sado-masochistic relationship, in the second the power of the super-ego is invested in the narcissistic object whose love and approval becomes a matter of life and death. The later development and outcome of the two analyses conformed with the designation I have given them. They both profited from their analyses in terms of developments in their lives, but the second patient gained significantly more capacity to use her mind creatively and freely. In the first case the analysis was charac-terised by intense negative therapeutic reactions and severe attacks on the analyst's capacity to work; progress and gain was followed by resentment that this depended on her attending for analysis and that the analyst had not enabled the patient to do it for herself. The second case was characterised by a defensive distancing and fear of the analyst becoming supremely powerful. This gradually gave way to a full play of positive and negative transference phenomena. It was important in this case to keep in mind that, whilst drawing attention to the patient's avoidance of a parental transference by the cultivation of an alternative narcissistic relationship, this was the best the patient could do until her fears of that super-ego relationship abated.

The backgrounds of these two patients were similar. Both had divorced parents; both had mothers with difficulties in their maternal function and both had successful fathers noted for their ruthless self-centredness. However, these features were much grosser in the parents of the patient whose disorder was predominantly libidinal and defensive. She was considerably less disturbed and less egocentric than either of her parents, whereas the patient suffering from a predominantly destructive narcissistic disorder was significantly more disturbed than either of her parents. One can see a generational escalation in her case in contrast to a generational de-escalation in the other.

I am suggesting that in both cases a narcissistic object relationship produces a twinship in fact or phantasy. In the first case it results in something like the infamous Bonnie and Clyde, and in the second something like Romeo and Juliet. Death lurks in both scenarios, but in one the partnership is based on a shared love of killing; in the other death is preferred to a life without the other's love. Such is the extent of projective identification in the narcissistic relationship of Romeo and Juliet that life without the other seems impossible. Bonnie and Clyde also are psychic twins but united by mutual murderousness.

CONCLUSION

In summary what I am suggesting is that narcissistic disorders arise when an ego-destructive super-ego has arisen in the course of development. Following Bion (1959,1962) I think that this results from a failure of "containment" in infancy; an inter-subjective failure of correspondence; sometimes predominantly due to factors in the mother and sometimes in the infant. A narcissistic organisation evolves, using narcissistic object relationships, internal, external, or both, to evade the resultant hostile super-ego. This may produce a predominantly libidinal or a predominantly destructive narcissistic organisation. I further suggested that the libidinal, defensive, organisation is most likely to arise when the main factor in the original failure of containment is on the parental side and the destructive organisation when the major factor is an excess of object-hostility in the infant. If we use the word narcissism to denote an urge to annihilate the otherness of the object, the answer to the question, what part does narcissism play in narcissistic disorders, is that it depends on how destructive they are. If the organisation is predominantly destructive, narcissism as anti-object attachment appears to play a large part; if it is predominantly libidinal then infantile and childhood trauma appears to play the larger part

References

Abraham, K. (1908) 'The Psycho-Sexual Differences between Hysteria and Dementia Praecox', in trans. D. Bryan and A. Strachey *Selected Papers of Karl Abraham* (1973), London: Hogarth Press, 64–79.

Abraham, K. (1917) 'Ejaculatio Praecox', in trans. D. Bryan and A. Strachey *Selected Papers of Karl Abraham* (1973), London: Hogarth Press, 64–79.

Abraham, K. (1919) 'A Particular Form of Neurotic Resistance against the Psycho-Analytic Method', in trans. D. Bryan and A. Strachey *Selected Papers of Karl Abraham* (1927), London: Hogarth Press, 303–11.

Abraham, K. (1924) 'A Short Study of the Development of the Libido, Viewed in the Light of the Mental Disorders', in trans. D. Bryan and A. Strachey *Selected Papers of Karl Abraham* (1927), London: Hogarth Press, 418–501.

Bion, W. R. (1959) 'Attacks on Linking', in *Second Thoughts* (1967), New York: Jason Aronson, 93–109.

Bion, W. R. (1962) *Learning from Experience*, London: Heinemann.

Britton, R. (2003) *Sex, Death, and the Superego*, London: Karnac Books.

Freud, S. (1905) 'Three Essays on the Theory of Sexuality', in *SE*, vol. VII, 125–44.

Freud, S. (1914) 'On Narcissism', in *SE*, vol. XIV, 73–102.

Horney, K. (1936) 'The Problem of the Negative Therapeutic Reaction', in *Psychoanalytic Quarterly*, vol. 5, 29–44.

O'Shaughnessy, E. (1999) 'Relating to the Superego', in *International Journal of Psychoanalysis*, vol. 69, 457–70.

Radice, B. (1973) *Who's Who in the Ancient World*, London: Penguin Books.

Rey, J. H. (1979) 'Schizoid Phenomena in the Borderline', in J. Le Boit and A. Capponi (eds), *Advances in the Psychotherapy of the Borderline Patient*, New York: Jason Aronson, 449–84.

Riviere, J. (1936) 'A Contribution to the Analysis of the Negative Therapeutic Reaction', in *International Journal of Psychoanalysis*, vol. 17, 304.

Rosenfeld, H. R. (1964) 'On the Psychopathology of Narcissism', in *Psychotic States: A Psycho-Analytical Approach* (1965), New York: International Universities Press, 169–79.

Rosenfeld, H. R. (1971) 'A Clinical Approach to the Psychoanalytic Theory of the Life and Death Instincts: An Investigation into the Aggressive Aspects of Narcissism', in *International Journal of Psychoanalysis*, vol. 52, 169–78.

Rosenfeld, H. R. (1987) *Impasse and Interpretation*, London: Routledge.

Segal, H. (1997) 'Some Implications of Melanie Klein's Work: Emergence from Narcissism', in J. Steiner (ed.), *Psychoanalysis, Literature and War*, London: Routledge, 75–85.

Steiner, J. (1987) 'The Interplay between Pathological Organisations and the Paranoid–Schizoid and Depressive Positions', in *International Journal of Psychoanalysis*, vol. 68, 69–80.

Chapter 4

Discussion of Ron Britton's paper

Hanna Segal

Of the various possible approaches to the problems of narcissism, Ron decided to centre his paper on the role of narcissism in personality disorders. I shall follow suit, since it is in this area that Herbert Rosenfeld made his fundamental contribution to problems of narcissism. In his 1971 paper he linked narcissism to the death instinct and described the narcissistic organisation – a narcissistic structure which is both a defence against and an implication of the death instinct and its manifestation in envy. As in all such organisations both libidinal and destructive elements, of course, play a role. In his later work Herbert tried to distinguish between what he called libidinal narcissism and destructive narcissism. I think his description of destructive narcissism, a structure based on projective identification with an internal object which dominates the personality (as, for example, in his classic description of the gang), is generally accepted as uncontroversial and has inspired much of our later work. But this is not the case in relation to his description of libidinal narcissism. There are some disagreements about the actual interplay of the libidinal and destructive forces in narcissism.

Ron describes Rosenfeld's view, as expressed by him in many papers, that it is important to distinguish "between those narcissistic states in which the libidinal aspects predominate, from those where the destructive aspects of narcissism predominate". He refers to my views saying, "for her there is only destructive narcissism and libidinal narcissism doesn't exist". This is not quite correct. When I state that I do not believe in a persistent libidinal narcissism, i.e. a libidinal narcissism as part of a narcissistic structure, what I actually mean is this: Klein differentiates between what she calls narcissistic states and what she calls narcissistic object relations but what she actually means, quite clearly, is a narcissistic structure, since those object relations are internalised. The narcissistic state is an identification with the original ideal object. This is a temporary state because in non-pathological development the ideal object becomes a good object. If the ideal object is felt as good and strong enough then there is less need to project everything bad outside – projections are gradually withdrawn and the ideal object becomes an ordinary good object. This kind of libidinal narcissism, therefore, is only a passing phase. Of course, like all infantile states it does not entirely disappear and reappears now and again in our adult life, for instance in states of being in love which often contains a strong narcissistic element. And indeed how impoverished our lives would be if we didn't experience such states. But if the state of being in love does not evolve into more mature loving then we are in trouble. Though Oscar Wilde says that the man who falls in love with himself has a happy love affair for the rest of his life, in actual fact he wasn't that happy.

Ron quotes Romeo and Juliet as an example of libidinal narcissism but that too ends in self-destruction and death. Rosenfeld says about destructive narcissism, quoted by Ron, "death is idealised as a solution to all problems". He applies it only to what he calls destructive narcissism but it seems equally true of the so-called libidinal narcissism. It sounds as though I was saying that all narcissistic patients are the same. Of course they are not. But where Rosenfeld, and I take it that Ron agrees with him, sees libidinal narcissism as a situation in which libido predominates over the destructive part, I see that in some cases the death instinct is more powerful and dominates over the life instinct and in other cases less so.

It is evident that of Ron's two cases the first patient is very much iller. Nearly her whole personality is dominated by her narcissistic organisation. His second case is very much less so. She has a clearly idealised and highly eroticised relation to her twin but the question is why the narcissistic structure or organisation at all? What is kept at bay? She obviously has a much healthier ego and she has a job, husband, family but such libido as is destined to become part of the narcissistic structure impoverishes the rest of her life.

Ron refers to John Steiner's concept of the pathological organisation – at basis a narcissistic one which is a structure defending both against the paranoid schizoid anxiety and the depressive one. I think of prime importance is which predominates. It is quite clear that Ron's first patient is struggling with most primitive oral sadistic paranoid anxieties. The second patient seemed to be defending more against oppressive and Oedipal anxieties.

The second point I want to raise is the problem of the super ego. Ron quotes Rosenfeld, saying that at the centre of the narcissistic structure is an envious, destructive super ego. Ron says about both his patients that they were struggling against a murderous super ego. First, I question why the object is described as a super ego. Do we now call all internal objects super ego? In the case of Ron's first patient I would think of a persecutory object. I think I call super ego only that aspect of the internal object which exercises moral pressure though its roots, as we know, may be in the persecutory or ideal object. I think of the super ego as bad when it is filled with hatred, of course, but also as not a good super ego if it is over-loving. I see a good super ego being more like a litmus paper – reality sense in the moral sphere – and it should not be part of any power structure. It does not tell you what to do – only what is. Also, in some places Ron refers to it being a paternal super ego – a third object – but it is clear in his first case, and he says so, that it is much more primitive anxieties that are in play and invade the Oedipal theme.

Why is the envious murderous super ego taken almost for granted by both Rosenfeld and Ron Britton? After all, the narcissistic person lives in a hall of mirrors. Isn't this murderous super ego, in part at least, a projection of the patient's own feelings? Describing a patient, Peter, in *Impasse and Interpretation* Herbert Rosenfeld speaks of the murderousness of his envy. So what is the narcissistic structure defending against? The object's murderousness or the subject's? Confusion. Rosenfeld has emphasised that somewhere at the base there is a failure of splitting. Britton accepts this view, and so do I, that defences against confusion are paramount. But we do know that the most powerful element in confusion is envy. If you hate a bad object and love a good object you know where you are. But if you hate and project the hate and the envy into the good object then you are bound to be confused because the better the object is the quicker it turns into a bad object filled with projections. Narcissistic organisations protect us from that confusion. Ron emphasises the role of the failure of containment and also the role played by parental projections. This, of course, is very important but equally, and in some ways maybe more, important is what is being projected into the container.

Which takes us to the whole question of the relative importance between external and internal factors. It is significant that the parents of the iller of the two patients were in fact less awful than the parents of the second patient. Therefore, we can assume that her projections were more violent and disruptive. In fact, her dream of feeding the baby for which she blames her mother could well be her own ferocious envious attack on the feeding process. All three of us – Rosenfeld, Britton and I – have observed that paradoxically it is the better environment that gives a worse prognosis, except in extreme cases and this emphasises the importance of the internal factors (while not, of course, ignoring the interplay with the environment).

I do not think Rosenfeld would agree but it is my impression that, in fact, he got more and more preoccupied with the traumatic factor than with the reality of the patient's or child's part in this process. Looking at the sessions reported by Ron I have a feeling that more attention is paid to the lack of containment and the fear of the bad super ego than to the patient's projections.

I want to end on a free association of mine. For some reason, as I was reading these sessions, an old joke came to my mind. At a party an old lady overheard a conversation between some young people about sex. She listened attentively then called a young man aside and whispered "doesn't anybody now ever do it the old fashioned way?" I suddenly had a picture of myself as this old lady asking shyly "doesn't anybody ever nowadays do it the old fashioned way and interpret straight envy?" I think this joke has a point. I think of all situations the hardest one to bear for the patient is the realisation of his primitive envy. It is also the most frightening and hardest thing for the analyst to deal with and we have endless ways of avoiding it.

Reference

Rosenfeld, H. A. (1971) 'A Clinical Approach to the Psychoanalytic Theory of the Life and Death Instincts: An Investigation into the Aggressive Aspects of Narcissism', in *International Journal of Psychoanalysis*, vol. 52, 169–78.

Chapter 5

Some notes on H. A. Rosenfeld's contributions to psychoanalysis

Riccardo Steiner[1]

'Ich binn kein Theoretiker'. Those were the words with which Rosenfeld wanted to underline his way of being a psychoanalyst during the first interview I had with him and which is now lost in the night of time. That Saturday morning at the beginning of March, it suddenly started snowing and while he was telling me this, for a brief moment, Rosenfeld looked outside the bay window of his house in Woronzov Road, London, at the roses in his front garden as if he was rather worried about the snow they had to bear. Then, slowly, he turned his head and eyes towards me, as if curious to see the effect his words were having on me, being from the Continent and having just arrived the day before, and speaking to him about the so-called revolutionary experience of the late 1960s, where everything was practice but in reality was also a rather odd theory. The expression on his face lit up with one of those smiles that everybody who has met him, I think, still remembers; a smile which seemed never ending in wrinkling his spacious forehead, lengthening his lips and the whole mouth, with rather strong teeth emerging, whilst at the same time his eyes, half open, where one could sense a sly blitz full of ironic undertones, watched mine with a sort of benevolent patience, as if to say: 'Well, this is me . . . it is up to you to see what you want to do or to choose . . .'.

It did not cross my mind in those days that I might, one day, be asked to contribute to illustrate certain aspects of his work. Believe me, it is not an easy task; there are my difficulties – well known to all those who know me – such as never finding enough time to write a short paper. However, there is something else: in spite of Rosenfeld's statements, which at first seem to facilitate the task for those who have to illustrate his work, his claim not to be a theoretician is, in reality, a theoretical position in its own way, which needs to be understood in its own specificity and in the problems which arise from it.

1 I would like to thank Jenny Itzcovitz and Tim Long for their careful editing of this paper.

Rosenfeld left two books. The first, *Psychotic States* (1965) is today considered pioneering research in the field of psychotic states. The second, *Impasse and Interpretation* (1987), published after his death, illustrates Rosenfeld's further research on psychosis, on the therapeutic impasse and on dealing with difficult cases not necessarily psychotic. It also details his views concerning projective identification, negative therapeutic reactions, libidinal and destructive narcissism and the role played by preverbal traumatic experiences in many disturbances in patients, his changed views about the technique to adopt in dealing with difficult cases as well as, finally, the role played by the personality and mistakes of the analyst in facilitating, disturbing and sometimes even in disrupting treatment. All those issues occupied Rosenfeld's attention during the last fifteen to twenty years of his career. Some of those views have been considered highly controversial, particularly by his Kleinian colleagues here in London (see also J. Steiner in this book).

As a result of his sudden death in 1986 at the age of seventy-five, when he was still in full practice, the second book also contains notes and after-thoughts on various issues which Rosenfeld was still elaborating (he was unable to correct the final proofs of the book). In addition to what has been published in his books and in some periodicals, there remain in his archives endless notes, seminars, supervisions and lectures that Rosenfeld gave in America, but particularly in Europe – Germany, France, Italy and so on – during the last fifteen years of his life, travelling there regularly and perhaps even too much. Some of this material has been taped and his Italian colleagues, for instance, published an extremely vivacious book on his supervisions that was translated into English (De Masi 2001). However, much of this material remains unpublished due to the difficulty in collating it. In the archives here in London there are many clinical cases that are still in the form in which Rosenfeld presented them, mainly abroad, but the material is extremely transparent and for reasons of confidentiality they should remain unpublished.

All this material reveals to us that Rosenfeld was obviously an enthusi-astic propagator of his and his colleagues' ideas, but one also has the impression that some of the thoughts and ideas expressed in the material were the result of an ongoing process of sedimentation in Rosenfeld's mind – a 'work in progress' so to speak – and as such can be put together today in meaningful and definitive form only with great difficulty.

Furthermore, besides being extremely valuable evidence of the way an analyst like Rosenfeld worked on his clinical material, if one considers all these notes, the extremely detailed cases (and those who collated his clinical material will remember the enormous folders containing years and years of analysis of patients that Rosenfeld probably wrote at night) one gets the impression, and I do not think it is only my misinterpretation, of a sort of disproportion between what Rosenfeld actually published and what he wrote, observed, noticed or even spoke about in private. When at his best, his capacity for identification with the patient was such that he seemed able to, and determined to, collect and make sense of nearly everything the patient was able to communicate, or even not communicate, to him or to the person he was supervising. One is often reminded of the short story by Borges (1975), *Del rigor en la Ciencia* (On Exactitude in Science), on the problems related to translation in which he imagines cartographers who wish to create the most precise map of their empire and end up with a map that is the exact same size as the empire itself.

I say all this to try to further clarify what I would like to say concerning Rosenfeld's characteristics as an analyst. And, certainly, much could be said even regarding his passion for detailed bibliography, although some people thought it was too much like the typical obsession for encompassing precision of an old-fashioned German scholar. I know I have the same bad habit, but Rosenfeld was not responsible for it.

Rosenfeld did not have the philosophical and epistemological interests of Bion and the taste for expressing himself in Bion's inimitable mixture of styles: scientific, literary 'à la Beckett', the philosophical style of the Oxford analytic philosopher and the rhapsodic style of the mystics. He did not invent concise labels for concepts, such as the expressions 'alpha/beta function', 'reverie' and 'container' that are repeated by everybody and are now almost iconic symbols of expression. Nor did Rosenfeld have the synthetic, poetic mastery of Segal's clinical writing or the variety of her extra-analytical interests, which are an intrinsic part of her thinking.

Nevertheless, Rosenfeld, different as he was from these colleagues with whom he is very often remembered, contributed to the formation of that famous group of researchers on the primitive unconscious aspects and 'phantasies' of the self and its communication during the more than twenty years they worked together, in London, before Bion went to America in the 1970s. A Brazilian newspaper once called the London of those years a sort of 'Princeton of psychoanalysis', comparing the group's work with that of the great physicists who, before and during the 1950s, had left a landmark in the study of sub-atomic particles. Of course, analogies are always dangerous and too loose but there is something true in what has been stated.

Rosenfeld was a clinician gifted with a rare capacity for observation and perception of the so-called psychotic areas of our personality or for psychotic states as such. At times he reminded one of a sort of dowser of the psychotic areas or of the psychotic states, who could make use of hypersensitive, perceptive and intuitive antennae, and who got in touch with the patient, as if unconsciously breathing, listening and perceiving him with the whole of himself, without prejudice, particularly when dealing with those areas.

He frequently worked through a slow accumulation of very subtle details of his observations and perceptions, as if he had to immerse himself again and again in the material, to mentally speak to it, feeling it, metabolising it inside himself. And then, suddenly, he came out with an extremely quick note and observation and interpretation, sometimes using a sort of expressionistic dramatisation of the material in order to highlight the dominant unconscious affective and intellectual note of a session. It was Rosenfeld himself who referred to his preferred German expressionist painters. And when he spoke in German, that was particularly remarkable.

Due to his constantly being immersed in the clinical material of his and other patients, what strikes one in reading what he left us is the fact that his hypotheses and theoretical formulations are so organically bound to the clinical material that sometimes one has to rescue them, reading and rereading the enormous wealth of clinical observations, almost as if, to fully appreciate them, one has to perform Rosenfeld's process of observation and interaction with his patient, keeping in strict contact with the clinical material. In *Impasse and Interpretation* for instance, there are twenty-four clinical cases reported, comprising some of his own cases and others that he was supervising, and in *Psychotic States* there are thirteen clinical cases described. It is impossible to make sense of them all in a short article.

What I have tried to do is to refresh the reader's memory of Rosenfeld's work, choosing a few themes only. It goes without saying that this is a personal choice open to criticism and enrichment.

Where shall I start? I don't think it is difficult to imagine it and even my illustrious, homonymous colleague J. Steiner, in speaking of H. Segal's eightieth birthday, referred rightly so to the years of the immediate-post-Second-World-War period in London. But in Rosenfeld's case, I would also draw your attention to the significance of the years 1940–45, because it was during those years that the archives of the British Psychoanalytical Society tell us that he had applied for training. After having emigrated to England quite early in 1935 to escape from Nazi Germany, Rosenfeld worked for years in English hospitals and mental hospitals and one should contextualise this work thinking of the way mental patients were treated at the time and even later on in mental hospitals in Great Britain. Rosenfeld will touch more than once in his work on the management problems related to psychotic patients. Indeed, this is a very important chapter of Rosenfeld's work and of those who, influenced by him, are still trying to treat psychotic patients privately and in hospitals, of their hopes and of the political and administrative difficulties they have to face. But to go back for a moment to the young Rosenfeld, I would like to highlight the significance of the month of March 1944. It was the month in which Klein submitted her paper during the Controversial Discussions, 'The Emotional Life and Ego Development of the Infant' (King and Steiner 1992), but also the month in which Rosenfeld started to treat what he then called the case of 'Mildred'.

Mildred was a patient who, during her analysis as a training case of Rosenfeld, had a psychotic breakdown characterised by what Rosenfeld called a schizophrenic state with depersonalisation. In treating Mildred, and in starting to understand her problems, Rosenfeld was able to publish a paper in 1947 that immediately drew quite a lot of attention to his work because, using pure psychoanalytical interpretations and without changing the parameters of the setting or introducing reassurances or other ways to deal with her disturbances, Rosenfeld managed to treat Mildred quite successfully, something that most of the analytical community of the time thought impossible and very problematic (remember for instance Freud's attitude concerning the treatment of psychosis). Mildred's case therefore was published only a few months after Klein had in 1946 published her landmark paper 'Notes on Some Schizoid Mechanisms', which really opened up a new era in psychoanalysis. Many of Rosenfeld's observations concerning the way Mildred was splitting but also, do not forget, fragmenting her ego and projecting it outside, into others and into Rosenfeld, and many of Rosenfeld's observations on all her difficulties in introjecting, during her psychotic state, nearly overlap, although with some differences with Klein's paper of 1946.

It is impossible for me to comment on Rosenfeld's statement that M. Klein did not want him to publish his observations on Mildred's case and the way she used projective identification before she had published her own paper on the subject, except to confirm that that is what he told me and others (see also J. Steiner in this book). I therefore would like just to stress here the importance that Klein's 1946 paper had for Rosenfeld. Had I the time, as I mentioned earlier, I could demonstrate the importance of Klein's 1944 paper to Mildred's case, particularly regarding Klein's descriptions of secondary narcissism, the necessary up to a point withdrawal of the baby inside an idealised object. One has just to think of her further observations during the discussion of her paper with E. Sharpe for instance (King and Steiner 1992: 776–8).

Furthermore, ideally one should consider the whole context of those years, including the work of P. Heimann, J. Riviere and M. Balint, and the observations of Winnicott on integrated ego states versus disintegrated states and so on. But one factor has to be particularly stressed: Rosenfeld, like many of those who started their career during those years, besides of course Klein and her colleagues, had a passionate relationship with Freud's later views (1914, 1917, 1920, 1923, 1926, 1933, 1940). Rosenfeld went on referring to him and speaking in a language that was often strictly Freudian until the end of his career; see for instance how in *Impasse and Interpretation* (1987) he rediscussed Freud's views concerning the fusion and defusion of the drives and what he, Rosenfeld, called pathological fusion, all issues he had already started discussing in his seminal paper on destructive narcissism (1971a). If one looks at Heimann's, Isaacs' as well as Klein's papers during the Controversial Discussions, you could see how much these issues were in the foreground (King and Steiner 1992: 742–4).

Without doubt, it was a polemic, passionate relationship. A few years had just passed since Freud's death in 1939 and his daughter's attitude did not make things very easy for Klein and her young pupils. Faced today with all sorts of new vistas, our relationship with Freud has changed significantly. Yet what is happening today often reminds me of what M. Klein wrote to Jones in the spring of 1941 (King and Steiner 1992; 231) when she described the creative shock created in her by her reading of Freud's 'The Ego and the Id' (1923b) and the disaffection of her colleagues for Freud's deep thinking: 'Analysts, like fish, prefer to swim on the surface'. Yet I have to say that it is my impression that without considering that deep, passionate, even if polemic, contact with Freud's deepest implications concerning the boundaries between the biological and the psychical, many of Rosenfeld's contributions would also be unthinkable.

ROSENFELD'S VIEWS ON THE SPLITTING AND FRAGMENTATION OF THE EGO

I have chosen the case of Mildred as a sort of reference point and a springboard to try and illustrate how some of Rosenfeld's views came about and overall how they developed in time. This method of proceeding has its own advantages and disadvantages. One advantage is that it helps me not to lose myself in following all Rosenfeld's papers chronologically. The disadvantage is that there could be the risk that I want to demonstrate that everything was already there in Mildred's case, thereby shrinking Rosenfeld's development into one single case as in a sort of grotesque concertino.

Please do not misunderstand me: some of Rosenfeld's latest developments contained, for instance, in *Impasse and Interpretation* in his after-thoughts are not found in Mildred's case. Yet in rereading it, it seems to me possible to show that in spite of the enormous richness of the clinical details of Rosenfeld's case material and the Talmudic subtleties with which he elaborated his observations through subtle variations and accumulations through time, and besides the danger of losing oneself in all this material, there is also a structural coherence of interests and even of themes in Rosenfeld's work that, if one uses Mildred as I tried to do, emerges with outstanding clarity.

Mildred, as I said, was the training case of Rosenfeld and came to analysis because of so many somatic symptoms. But after a few months she became increasingly silent and her schizoid symptoms and detachments from her feelings developed into a real state of depersonalisation. She began to feel more and more dim, sleepy and semi-unconscious during the sessions and outside. Even the technical handling of the treatment became difficult: she could not come to the sessions or spent hours and hours putting herself together in the morning to prepare herself for the sessions because she had lost contact with the continuity of her life and each gesture became fragmented, isolated one from the other (they were 'action thoughts' as Rosenfeld called them) and she could not remember the sequence of them and so on. It was, incidentally, through this case that Rosenfeld was able to link depersonalisation to the fragmentation of the self, typical of schizophrenia. I cannot go into further detail except to say that at one point it became clear to Rosenfeld that all this was accompanied by enormous paranoid anxieties, which started emerging in the transference. Rosenfeld did not know what to do at first but, pushed by his wish to understand and by a sort of creative curiosity, and using at the same time what he was learning in his analysis with M. Klein, felt he had to go on treating the patient against the advice of his supervisor. Let's stop here for a moment.

Here one can find something typical of Rosenfeld that, if one follows the whole of his career, you could observe in many of his other papers on the subject, also because he returned to the Mildred case again and again until the end of his life. One has simply to read the introductory notes in *Impasse and Interpretation*. Tall, very thin and seemingly a bit shy, gifted with a subtle sense of irony, particularly when confronted with issues related to psychotic states, Rosenfeld had the capacity to endure uncertainty and to come back to tackle the symptoms, and a quite uncommon sense of determination driven by the typical creative curiosity of those who leave a mark in their field of research. He never seemed to give up, to the extent that his conviction and enthusiasms could be excessive, particularly in his later years. In treating Mildred he found himself facing unknown territory, but he was determined to explore, understand and chart it.

As he himself said in his autobiographical notes, in the beginning he felt alone and isolated in treating psychotics, but after two to three years he drew enormous support from H. Segal's case of the treatment of schizophrenic patients already diagnosed as such at the beginning of the treatment (1950) and then from Bion's contributions (Bion 1967) and from the interest shown by colleagues abroad and in England too. But if one wants to understand that 'something' that distinguished Rosenfeld in the treatment of psychotic states (although he was not working alone in this area) one can see it already emerging very clearly in the case of Mildred. Let us go back to Mildred's own descriptions of the splitting of her ego in two and then to her further fragmentations and to Rosenfeld's statements that he gradually began to realise the specificity of the schizoid processes affecting Mildred, which seemed to affect the very core of her ego. You just have to imagine Rosenfeld gradually immersing himself not only in the splitting but in the fragmentation of Mildred and gradually trying to make sense of it, slowing down the process as he was used to doing, piece by piece, as if putting together a jigsaw puzzle, finding the fragments one by one and describing them to the patients. For those who worked with him in supervision, maybe they can remember the movement of his eyes, his slightly amused tone of voice in retracing the fragments, and the movement of his head and the curious expression on his face, intently focused in the effort to comprehend the various pieces, one way or another. At times, even his body movement and his long hands became part of the effort he was expressing, as if he wanted to physically pick up the fragments.

If we bear in mind Rosenfeld's statements concerning 'the very core of the ego' of Mildred and we look particularly at the papers that he wrote during the 1950s and 1960s, but also bear in mind the numerous observations he made concerning how to handle the disturbances of psychotic patients in *Impasse and Interpretation*, we could easily see that the more and more refined study of the core fragmentation of the ego of the patient will be one of the most important contributions that Rosenfeld will have made in this area of the understanding and treatment of psychosis. He will use his observations to also understand drug addiction, hypochondria and psychosomatic illnesses.[2] He will then use his observations and experience to also treat less disturbed types of patient, such as borderline ones. What he will sometimes underline is a rather new angle from which to study those phenomena. Remember Rosenfeld's 1949 paper 'Notes on the Psychopathology of Confusional States in Chronic Schizophrenia', republished in 1965 in *Psychotic States*, which is often forgotten.

As I have already said – and the same is valid for H. Segal's or Bion's early contributions – Rosenfeld's work on the splitting and fragmentation was dependent on what Klein (1946) had observed happening in the baby during what, in this paper, Klein started calling the 'schizoparanoid phase preceding repression and the depressive position'. Yet, in the paper I just mentioned, Rosenfeld described a specific phenomenon; the enormous, rigid, violent splitting one can find in psychotic patients as a defence against confusion, the confusional states, the simultaneous confusional presence of hate and love, inside, outside, feeling alive and death, which is so unbearable for those kinds of patients, as if one is faced with the emergence of the primary process and its logic. Klein (1957) will later on stress that this rigid splitting was determined by the avoidance of envy, but Rosenfeld was never completely persuaded by that.

What is of utmost importance is that Rosenfeld also described the alternatives one has to face when the splitting lessens. It can lead to integration but also to a sort of chaotic catastrophic implosion, a global unmanageable

2 See in *Psychotic States* (1965): 'Notes of the Psychoanalysis of the Superego – Conflict in an Acute Schizophrenic Patient' (1952), 'Consideration Regarding the Psychoanalytical Approach to Acute and Chronic Schizophrenia' (1954), 'On Drug Addiction' (1960), 'Notes on Psychopathology and Psychoanalytic Treatment of Schizophrenia' (1963) and also 'The Psychopathology of Hypochondria' (1964).

disorder of the self of the patient, who then desperately tries to get rid of, to evacuate in terms of Bion's model of the mind, the confusion itself, escalating the process of fragmentation and disorder due to what Bion called 'nameless dread'. One wonders whether Bion's bizarre objects and some of his differentiations between projection and evacuation did not find some sources of inspiration in Rosenfeld's views, as Rosenfeld himself claimed later on in his paper 'On the Psychopathology and Treatment of Psychotic Patients' (1981). As I will try to show briefly, even in his later years Rosenfeld seemed to lack the brilliant synthetic formulations of his colleagues to make sense of the material, but at the same time he was describing the phenomena in great detail. One should also not forget, and here the analogy with the sub-atomic physics has a certain ground of truth, that Rosenfeld and all those who were working, and are still working today, with psychotics are confronted with the massiveness and enormous violence of phenomena, which besides requiring certain specific capacities from the analyst, often were, and still are, quite new and obscure and need extremely careful observations and formulations and differentiations.

ROSENFELD'S EXPLORATION OF VARIOUS TYPES OF PROJECTIVE AND INTROJECTIVE IDENTIFICATIONS

But how does this kind of splitting and fragmentation manifest itself?

As we now know, a major role is played by projective and introjective identification, which can be observed and felt by the analyst in the transference and countertransference working with those patients. But the same experience to a certain degree is observable with less disturbed patients. Mildred contains some of the core observations of this. Let us start with the transference.

At one point already in this paper Rosenfeld describes a particular kind of transference that he called 'delusional'. Mildred feared being totally intruded and changed into another person by Rosenfeld. He would later term this 'psychotic transference', 'schizophrenic transference' and so on, which reflects the kind of primitive object relationships of those patients and therefore, contrary to what Freud thought, it is a transference, although of a particular kind. From Mildred's case onwards, Rosenfeld will insist all his professional life on the characteristics of this transference.[3] Therefore it is

---

3 See the following papers in *Psychotic States* (1965): 'Notes on the Psychoanalysis of the Super Ego – Conflict in an Acute Schizophrenic Patient' (1952), 'Transference Phenomena and Transference Analysis of an Acute Catatonic Patient' (1954) and the conclusive 'Notes on the Psychopathology and Treatment of Schizophrenia' (1963).

possible to trace a very clear line of continuity between Mildred and the cases Rosenfeld discusses in *Impasse and Interpretation* (1987), whether they belonged to his own patients or those he supervised.

Why was Rosenfeld so interested in insisting on the specificity of this transference? Because, among other characteristics, it is strongly erotised, although the analyst has to be aware of its nature and not to interpret the material at an Oedipal level as it might appear, because of the primitive way of functioning of those patients – what Rosenfeld, from Mildred's case onwards, called the 'concreteness' of their functioning. In these cases, the patient takes the interpretation as an invitation to act, or as a seduction and everything becomes unmanageable. But all this can be understood in the transference and counter-transference, if one is aware, according to Rosenfeld, of the very important role played by the primitiveness of the massive projective and introjective identification of the patient, and that was the case with Mildred.

It is also interesting that in describing her way of avoiding her feelings, Rosenfeld more than once mentioned envy and the way Mildred was projecting it, thereby impoverishing her way of thinking. The avoidance and projection of massive quantities of envy will be at the core of one of Rosenfeld's masterpieces, to which I have already referred more than once, the description of the primitive murderous superego of a schizophrenic patient in a paper published in 1952, which was part of the *Festschrift* in honour of M. Klein. Here, Rosenfeld mentioned also 'primary' envy, the envy for life itself, coming from this patient with whom he engaged in a sort of dialogue which at times reminds one of a mixture of Beckett and, as for the images used, of Bosch and M. Ernst. I do not know whether the reader remembers when Rosenfeld describes the patient shouting inarticulated monosyllables or disconnected words and the way he managed to make sense of them.

Again, it is obvious here that he had adopted the suggestions of Klein, who published *Envy and Gratitude* in 1957, but later on he will be helped enormously in his further formulations of the reasons why the patients who are dominated by excessive envy cannot think properly, not only by Bion's research and formulations but also by H. Segal's paper on the difference between 'symbolic equation and symbolisation' (1957), which made psychoanalytical sense of Rosenfeld's research and use of Vigotsky's, Goldstein's and others' phenomenological studies on the concreteness and particular distortion of the logic of psychotic patients (see Rosenfeld 1965: 147).

During his last years, as he wrote in *Impasse and Interpretation* (1987), Rosenfeld was no longer convinced that one should always give such central importance to the problems of envy. He insisted on the patient's vulnerability, on the risk of pathologising him if one insisted too much on interpreting envy in some cases (see also J. Steiner in this book). Perhaps the problem lies, as usual, in not mechanising and routinising interpretations based only on envy.

In connection with all of the above, I think I should point out something else which one will notice when reading Mildred's case. At one point, Rosenfeld clearly described a difference he observed in Mildred's projective identifications and that affected simultaneously her introjections. Mildred did not project only part of her ego but, when in an acute state, the projection and the fear of intrusion became so great that she tended to project the whole ego inside others or into Rosenfeld, at the same time being delusionally terrified of being totally possessed and changed by others and particularly by Rosenfeld. Rosenfeld will go on to re-examine (obviously supported particularly by Bion's sophisticated contributions and research, such as the notion of evacuation) the way projective identification works in psychosis, stressing its intense particular pathological and massive fragmenting quality. *And one can already see in the case of Mildred (1947) the importance attributed by Rosenfeld to the notion of massive projective identification, which is fundamental in understanding the concrete nature of the thinking of psychotic patients observed also by Segal in what she called 'symbolic equation'* (see Rosenfeld 1952 [1965]: 77).

For reasons of space, I cannot demonstrate here how this notion of massive or less massive projective identification could be further developed and could allow us to formulate a proper developmental process of projective and introjective identification (R. Steiner 1975, 1989a). What must be stressed, however, is that Mildred again shows the line of continuity in this area of Rosenfeld's research, which is probably one of the most interesting of his work. In an extremely condensed but important paper delivered to the CIBA Foundation in America for a symposium on psychosis in 1971, 'The Importance of Projective Identification in the Ego Structure and the Object Relation of Psychotic Patients' (1971b; see Chapter 10, this book), Rosenfeld at one point introduces a further observation concerning projective identification; among other types of projective identification he describes what he calls the 'parasitical projective identification' based again on an attempt by the patient to totally intrude and control the body and mind of his object, but this time in a silent, parasitical, passive way, to avoid any sort of feeling of dependency, envy, separation, anxiety and so on. The most difficult moment is encountered when the analyst is trying to make the patient aware of his parasitism. In this paper there is incredibly vivid clinical material referring to a patient who dreamt that his head was full of worms and wanted to transform Rosenfeld's head in this way too. In 1983, Rosenfeld will introduce a further type of projective identification, which he will call 'symbiotic projective identification', again trying to draw our attention to the differences between a state of total confusion with the object and a more benign state of fusion with the object where boundaries and differentiations are not totally lost.

As you can see, Rosenfeld used a process of accumulation that gives quite a rigorous coherence to his work in this area. Now, if we go back again to Mildred's paper, there is something else which is important to look at; more than once Rosenfeld, in describing her, mentioned the elusive quality of her communication, insisting on his necessity of interpreting her whole behaviour, particularly the non-verbal one, during her state of acute withdrawal, but he insisted also that at times Mildred was not only projecting her destructiveness and wish to control, but also good aspects of herself in order to protect them. He had to be very careful in order to understand all that and made several mistakes. Now, this is another area of Rosenfeld's research that one can see gradually emerging from Mildred's paper: his interest in the way the psychotic, but also the borderline patients he will study later on, try to communicate consciously and unconsciously and his attempt to differentiate the communicative aspects of projective identification, from the aggressive, destructive ones. Later on, through Bion's (1962) contributions on the differentiation between the psychotic and non-psychotic parts of the patient, his notion of containment, maternal reverie and some of the work of B. Joseph (1989), Rosenfeld became increasingly convinced of the importance of the subtle communicative aspects of projective identification.

I remember that once in a clinical seminar for candidates doing the membership course, Rosenfeld told a student: 'You see, you should use all your means of perception, even the pores of your skin if you can, to tune in with the patient'. Later on, particularly in many chapters of *Impasse and Interpretation* (1987), he became increasingly interested in describing the role played by the analyst and the impasses in the treatment created not only by the patient, but by the blind spots of the analyst not perceiving the patient's communications. One might disagree with some of his later statements, which appeared to support some of his patients too much, but one cannot deny the subtlety with which he tried to show the muddle created in analysis by misinterpreted non-verbal, and of course even verbal, communications, which can lead to serious impasses in the treatment.

Personally, I do not think one can entirely dismiss Rosenfeld's worries concerning the danger of retraumatising already traumatised patients with premature interpretations, insisting only on their wish to destroy the analyst and ignoring the communicative aspects of their projections, particularly when the history of the patient seems to indicate that the patient experienced massive and severe deprivations or traumas during the most vulnerable period of life, when verbal communication was not yet possible.

Rosenfeld was, and remained, very alert to the personal history of the patient throughout his professional career, thereby differentiating himself from some of his colleagues. The resort to statements such as 'well, in the end, all depends on the constitution of the patient' or the exclusive insistence, working in 'the here and now' on interpretations such as 'look what you do to me, who is so neutral and here to help you' using mainly one's own counter-transference, often seemed too superegoic, moralistic and omniscient to the late Rosenfeld, who insisted on the need for the analyst to remain open minded with regard to the history of the patient. However, I must emphasise that this is a very complex area, in which one has to also consider the major distortions and dangers inherent in the kind of 'chicken-soup analysis'[4] as I would call it, of those who are looking only for environmental deficits.

LIBIDINAL AND DESTRUCTIVE NARCISSISM

There is one final area of Rosenfeld's work on which I have to refresh the reader's memory, although I think in this case my task is made easier because probably at least one of his papers on the subject is very well known. I am referring to the one on 'Destructive Narcissism' (1971a), to give it its shorthand title, which according to J. Steiner 'although phrased in the now unfashionable language of "instinct theory", touches on a basic problem, which remains central to our understanding of severe psycho-pathology' (1993: 31). This paper, written for the International Congress of Psychoanalysis in Vienna in 1971, deeply influenced many of his colleagues here in London, such as M. Feldman, H. Rey, H. Segal, L. Sohn and J. Steiner, to mention just a few of them, and also many colleagues working abroad.

At this point, someone may ask: Does Mildred's case also contain Rosenfeld's views concerning destructive narcissism? Of course not! Yet, even in this case, Rosenfeld did not reach his latest observations just by chance. I already mentioned the importance of Klein's observations in the paper of 1944 during the Controversial Discussions on secondary narcissism, together for instance with all those interventions present also in Heimann's and Isaacs' papers during the Controversial Discussions on Freud's notions of fusion and defusion of instincts related to early object relationships, which will lead to Rosenfeld's notion of pathological fusion of instincts. This is at the core of what he means by 'destructive narcissism'. Indeed, he agrees with Freud that the death instinct can never be observed

---

4 The reader who is not acquainted with this expression and its comic meaning should remember that in the Jewish tradition, chicken soup is the soup that mothers usually keep prepared for whatever convenience or contingency. And there are many jokes concerning the readiness with which Jewish mothers feed and overfeed their babies and children, and even their husbands, with chicken soup when somebody in the family starts crying or complaining for whatever minor illness.

in a pure state[5] but manifests itself in destructive narcissism in a sort of pathological fusion with the libidinal instinct, which animates the phantasies related to a Mafia kind of organisation, the narcissistic organisation, a definition probably also inspired by Meltzer's contributions (1968), composed of various highly erotised and idealised aspects of the personality of the patient.

They obey the head of the Mafia and do not allow the more alive and dependent and reality-related parts of the personality of the patient to contact the analyst. The patient is under the enormous, hypnotic control of the Mafia and the whole structure is described by Rosenfeld as highly persuasive and seductively benign. If the patient obeys, apparently he lives in a state of peace, is promised all sorts of perverse gratifications and avoids envy, dependency and so on. But the whole omniscient, superior Mafia organisation pushes the patient towards greater and greater self-destructiveness, often of a suicidal kind, or to a complete oblivion of reality, of the parental intercourse, and to phantasies of having given birth to oneself. The analyst very often feels ignored, belittled and under the powerful hypnotic control of the Mafia. Only when the analyst gradually succeeds in lessening the control that the Mafia has on the patient, can he hope to have access to the more libidinal and dependent parts of the patient's personality and try to help him.

Of course, one should also refer to Rosenfeld's previous paper, 'On the Psychopathology of Narcissism' (1962; see Chapter 8, this book) in which he described the envious, superior identification of the narcissistic patient with the breast in order to avoid any pain and envious feelings, and in which he also called Freud's primary narcissism 'primary object relationships'. But do not forget that already in Mildred's case, Rosenfeld had very clearly described what he called her 'narcissistic withdrawal in a world of her own' as an alternative symptom to her depersonalisation . . . and he used words that remind one of what he will later describe in his papers on narcissism as the 'state of mind and the feelings of the narcissistic patient'. Much could be said about Mildred's fantasy concerning being controlled by a devil who did not allow people to move or escape and when they tried, the devil became even more controlling and persecuting. Rosenfeld had already

---

5 Curiously enough, in spite of his careful readings of Freud's latest work, Rosenfeld never came across or quoted the following statement contained in Freud's 'An Outline of Psycho-Analysis' (1940): 'We may picture an initial state as one in which the total available energy of Eros, which henceforward we shall speak of as "libido" is present in the still undifferentiated ego-id and serves to neutralize the destructive tendencies which are simultaneously present' (p. 149). In this case, the state of primary narcissism seems to contain both the death and the life drive and the life drive Eros, libido neutralising the death drive or destructive tendencies. I would suggest (R. Steiner 1989b) that in Freud's statement there are several hints at what Rosenfeld, and also A. Green, called destructive or death's narcissism.

related all this to the negative therapeutic reaction of Mildred following the views of J. Riviere but even later on he will stress the importance of the Mafia control on the patient as far as the negative therapeutic reaction is concerned (Rosenfeld 1987).

As you know, there were further problems and differentiations introduced by Rosenfeld concerning narcissism, such as thick-skinned and thin-skinned narcissistic patients (see Rosenfeld 1986, and also J. Steiner, Chapter 6, this book). For instance, one could ask oneself the following: What is the relationship between destructive narcissism and a highly erotised form of masochism? Or, what is the role played by a primitive disguised superego in destructive narcissism?[6]

And what about Rosenfeld's views concerning libidinal narcissism? He stressed the importance of the libidinal versus the destructive aspects of narcissism (1986) and tried also to justify in this way, with the differentiation between thin-skinned and thick-skinned narcissistic patients that I referred to earlier, some of his clinical ways of operating, particularly during his last years as an analyst (1986). It is, in my opinion and that of others, a rather complex area and I personally agree with H. Segal's views concerning libidinal narcissism. I remember having tried to discuss this with Rosenfeld, asking him how he would consider self-esteem coming from a fusion of a good part of the self and good introjections, but where envy should never be forgotten because some aspects of what he called 'libidinal narcissism' seemed to me too resemblant of Kohut's views. He reiterated his views on libidinal narcissism. I personally would have liked him to have had more time to develop many of his ideas, such as 'torso' in *Impasse and Interpretation* (1987), and discuss them with his colleagues. Incidentally, one has to contextualise Rosenfeld's research on narcissism in a particular Zeitgeist. Remember for instance Kohut's (1971, 1972) and Kernberg's (1975a, 1975b, 1984) views on the subject in America, and those of Grünberger (1966) and Green (1983, 1993) in France. Indeed, some of Rosenfeld's views on destructive narcissism and libidinal narcissism were very similar to those of Kernberg, but also of Green (R. Steiner 1987).

There is one last aspect of Rosenfeld's work that I would like to mention, albeit *en passant*. He did not have the extra-analytic interests of H. Segal for

---

6 Those were some of the issues I tried to discuss with Rosenfeld several times when I was still in analysis and even later on. Please do not misunderstand me, it is not that I claim that I had a direct influence on his thinking. It is nevertheless interesting that very recently, wanting to write a paper on masochism and its relations to destructive narcissism, I came across a paper by Rosenfeld which has not been quoted by anybody, appears to be almost unknown and was published after his death in a book, *Masochism*, entitled 'On Masochism: A theoretical and clinical approach', in which Rosenfeld tries to link masochism to his own views on destructive narcissism (pp. 151–74). Rosenfeld also speaks of a narcissistic envious superego in *Impasse and Interpretation* (1987).

instance, as I said earlier. Yet thinking of his work in connection with Segal's or even Bion's interest in the social field in groups and so on, one wonders how helpful it would be to apply to contemporary sociopolitical issues his views concerning, for instance, what happens when rigid splitting lessens and the danger that confusion can take over not only in the individual patients but on a larger social scale: the creation of a new chaotic and unmanageable disorder as a new order where all sorts of odd authoritarian solutions are then used to try to control all this. So many aspects of our present sociopolitical and institutional life, in all fields, remind us of this danger.

And what about Rosenfeld's views concerning the parasitical projective identification if applied do the pathology of institutional life or the way the welfare state has been and is still exploited in many countries? I personally tried to apply to sociopolitical issues some of Rosenfeld's views concerning what he called 'psychotic islands' present in our personality and described by him in a paper (1987) that I cannot discuss here in detail. Indeed, I mentioned the explosive danger represented by the Iraqi situation using Rosenfeld's notion of psychotic islands in discussing the increasing danger represented by the mishandlings by the West and the East of Saddam Hussein and the Iraqis, during the Congress on the sociopolitical involvement of psychoanalysis during the last century in July 1991, a few months before the explosion of the first Iraq war.

Rosenfeld himself tried to use his own ideas to understand sociopolitical phenomena. I have to confess that I tried to convince him more than once during my analysis, and later on, about the importance of his paper on destructive narcissism in order to understand some of the aspects of the Fascist and Nazi phenomena, particularly the role played by the narcissistic gang in collision with the head of the Mafia. Rosenfeld seemed to have slightly anticipated themes which became popular in the historiography of Fascism in Italy and Nazism in Germany (de Felice 1975), studying the collusive role played by the bureaucracy or even the population at large, with Mussolini and Hitler (Goldhagen 1996). I quoted the paper in a little anthology of Freud's work (R. Steiner 1973) when dealing with the paper on the psychology of the masses in 1973. But I had to deal with this in the transference of my analysis too! Yet I was very moved to discover that during the last two years of his life, Rosenfeld gave several seminars in Germany and also wrote a paper (1984) for a congress during which, at one point, he invited his German colleagues to try to understand some aspects of the Nazi regime using his ideas. The paper, which could be further developed because Rosenfeld only hinted at those issues, was never published in English but is available in German.

Thinking about what I said concerning some aspects of his last book, *Impasse and Interpretation*, and his other papers and projects, and of his sudden death, one perhaps could say that even for him, death was like a flower that blooms only once, as for all of us, but blooms like nothing else. It blooms when it wants: we do not have final control of it. Perhaps death came too soon, certainly abruptly, in the case of Rosenfeld, who nevertheless had lived a long and rich life. But what I have just said is perhaps one of those personal thoughts that are the result of one's own personal vicissitudes with this kind of flower.

While writing these notes, the title of a very beautiful, although now forgotten book, by an Italian writer, not Primo, but Carlo Levi, *Le parole sono pietre* (Words Are Stones 1955) sprang to mind. Actually, one could say that words are not only stones but also dates, and that years can become like heavy stones. I do not know whether I have really succeeded in lifting the weight of the more than twenty years that have passed since Rosenfeld's death, years during which one often had the impression that he had been, if not forgotten, at least put to one side. The passing of the millennium does not help either, because it seems to distance him, like so many other of our cultural ancestors, even further from us. But there must be a meaning in what the organisers of this meeting wanted to convey and the response of those who came here today speaks for itself. From my point of view, I would like to end by quoting, although rather imprecisely (I am getting old and my memory is from time to time imprecise) what W. Benjamin, probably one of the greatest cultural exponents of the German Jewish Diaspora of Rosenfeld's generation, wrote once concerning the poet and poetry. Benjamin did not agree with those who, speaking of a poet and his work, use the past tense, as in 'Rilke *was* a poet who . . .' and so on: a poet, when a genuine poet, must continue to be addressed, as with his work, using the present tense: 'Rilke *is* a poet who . . .'

Please do not misunderstand me! *Mutatis mutandis*, and maintaining a sense of proportion, I think that the same can be said of everybody who has left a creative mark in his field of activity or research. How much Rosenfeld *was* an analyst or still *is* an analyst, it is of course up to the reader to decide. I would just like to thank you for the patience with which you have read my notes.

References

Bion, W. (1962) *Learning from Experience*, London, Heinemann.

Bion, W. (1967) *Second Thoughts*, London, Heinemann.

Borges, J. L. (1975) 'On Exactitude in Science', in trans. N. T. de Giovanni, *A Universal History of Infamy*, London: Penguin Books.

De Felice, R. (1975) *Mussolini*, Torino: Einaudi.

De Masi, F. (ed.) (2001) *Herbert Rosenfeld at Work: The Italian Seminars*, London: Karnac Books.

Freud, S. (1914) 'On Narcissism: An Introduction', in *SE*, vol. 14, 73–102.

Freud, S. (1917) 'Mourning and Melancholia', in *SE*, vol. 14, 237–58.

Freud, S. (1920) 'Beyond the Pleasure Principle', in *SE*, vol. 18, 1–64.

Freud, S. (1923) 'The Ego and the Id', in *SE*, vol. 19, 13–66.

Freud, S. (1926) 'Inhibition Symptoms and Anxiety', in *SE*, vol. 20, 75–176.

Freud, S. (1933) 'New Lectures in Psychoanalysis', in *SE*, vol. 22, 1–182.

Freud, S. (1940) 'An Outline of Psycho-Analysis', in *SE*, vol. 23, 141–207.

Green, A. (1983) *Narcissisme de vie, narcissisme de mort*, Paris: P.U.F.

Green, A. (1993) *Le travail du negatif*, Paris: Ed. De Minuit.

Goldhagen, D. J. (1996) *Hitler's Willing Executioners: Ordinary Germans and the Holocaust*, New York: Knopf.

Grünberger, B. (1966) *Narcissism: Psychoanalytic Essays*, New York: International University Press.

Joseph, B. (1989) *Psychic Equilibrium and Psychic Change: Selected Papers of Betty Joseph*. M. Feldman and E. Bott Spillius (eds), London: Routledge.

Kernberg, O. (1975a) *Borderline Conditions and Pathological Narcissism*, New York: Jason Aronson.

Kernberg, O. (1975b) *Severe Personality Disorders*, New Haven and London: Yale University Press.

Kernberg, O. (1984) *Severe Personality Disorders: Psychotherapeutic Strategies*, New Haven, Conn.: Yale University Press.

King, P. and Steiner, R. (eds) (1992) *The Freud–Klein Controversies (1941–45)*, London: Routledge.

Klein, M. (1944) 'The Emotional Life and Ego Development of the Infant with Special Rreference to the Depressive Position', in P. King and R. Steiner (eds), *The Freud–Klein Controversies (1941–45)* (1992), London: Routledge, 752–97.

Klein, M. (1946) 'Notes on Some Schizoid Mechanisms', in *International Journal of Psychoanalysis*, vol. 27, 99–110.

Klein, M. (1957) *Envy and Gratitude*, London: Tavistock.

Kohut, H. (1971) *The Analysis of the Self*, New York: International University Press.

Kohut, H. (1972) 'Thoughts on Narcissism and Narcissistic Rage', in *Psychoanalytic Study of the Child*, vol. 27, 360–400.

Levi, C. (1955) *Le parole sono pietre* (Words are stones), Torino: Einaudi.

Meltzer, D. (1968) 'Terror, Persecution, Dread', in . . . *Sexual States of Mind*, Perthshire: Clunie Press, 99–106.

Rosenfeld, H. (1947) 'Analysis of Schizophrenic States with Depersonalization', in *Psychotic States* (1965), London: Hogarth Press, 13–33.

Rosenfeld, H. (1952) 'Notes on the Psychoanalysis of the Super Ego Conflict in an Acute Schizophrenic Patient', in *International Journal of Psychoanalysis*, vol. 33, 111–31; reprinted in *Psychotic States* (1965), London: Hogarth Press, 63–103.

Rosenfeld, H. (1965) *Psychotic States*, London: Hogarth Press.

Rosenfeld, H. A. (1971a) 'A Clinical Approach to the Psychoanalytic Theory of the Life and Death Instincts: An Investigation into the Aggressive Aspects of Narcissism', in *International Journal of Psychoanalysis*, vol. 52, 169–78.

Rosenfeld, H. A. (1971b) Contribution to the Psychopathology of Psychotic Patients. The Importance of Projective Identification in the Ego Structure and Object Relations of the Psychotic Patient', in P. Doucet and C. Laurin (eds), *Problems of Psychosis*, Amsterdam: Excerpta Medica; reprinted in E. Bott Spillius (ed.), *Melanie Klein Today. 1. Mainly Theory* (1988), London: Routledge, 117–37.

Rosenfeld, H. (1981) 'On the Psychopathology and Treatment of Psychotic Patients', in J. Grotstein (ed.), *"Do I Dare Disturb the Universe" A Memorial to W. R. Bion*, London: Karnac Books, 167–80.

Rosenfeld, H. (1984) 'Narzissmus und Aggression', in *Die psychoanalytische Haltung* (1988), Munchen Wien: Verlag Internationale Psychoanalyse, 375–91.

Rosenfeld, H. (1987) *Impasse and Interpretation*, London: Routledge.

Rosenfeld, H. (1988) 'On Masochism: A Theoretical and Clinical Approach', in R. A. Glick and D. I. Meyers (eds), *Masochism: Current Psychoanalytic Perspectives*, Hillsdale, London, Hove: The Analytic Press, 151–74.

Segal, H. (1950) 'Some Aspects of the Analysis of a Schizophrenic', in *International Journal of Psychoanalysis*, vol. 30, 268–78; reprinted in *The Work of Hanna Segal* (1981), New York: Jason Aronson, 101–20.

Segal, H. (1957) 'Notes on Symbol Formation', in *International Journal of Psychoanalysis*, vol. 38, 391–7; reprinted in *The Work of Hanna Segal* (1981), New York: Jason Aronson, 49–65.

Steiner, J. (1993) *Psychic Retreats*, London: Routledge.

Steiner, R. (1973) *Freud. Una antologia*, Napoli: Morano Editore.

Steiner, R. (1975) *Il Processo di Simbolizzazione Nell'Opera di Melanie Klein*, Torino: Boringhieri.

Steiner, R. (1987) 'Review of A. Green: *Narcissism de vie, narcissisme de mort*', in *International Journal of Psychoanalysis*, vol. 68, 133–7.

Steiner, R. (1989a) 'Review of J. Sandler Editor: *Projection, Identification, Projective Identification*', in *International Journal of Psychoanalysis*, vol. 70, 727–35.

Steiner, R. (1989b) 'On Narcissism: The Kleinian Approach', in O. Kernberg (ed.), *Psychiatric Clinics of North America*, vol. 12, 741–70.

Chapter 6

A personal review of Rosenfeld's contribution to clinical psychoanalysis

John Steiner

In this account of Herbert Rosenfeld's work I hope I can explain why he was not only a pioneer and innovator in a number of vital theoretical areas, but also in some ways one of the finest analysts and clinical teachers we have known. From his first paper in 1946 until his death forty years later he worked and wrote with astonishing energy and he left behind a formidable body of work. I think of the period 1946–78 as his classic period during which he became a recognised authority on the treatment of psychotic states by psychoanalysis. He showed that a psychotic transference can be observed and analysed and with Bion (1956, 1957, 1959), and Segal (1950, 1956), he created an atmosphere of initiative and experimentation in which a new understanding of psychosis could develop without requiring a change in the setting or in the analytic attitude towards patients. This area of his work is well known but I think his contribution to the treatment of less ill patients, particularly his work on schizoid states and on narcissism, his clinical insight, and his development of theory to support and sustain his analytic technique are not as recognised as they should be.

The obituary, written by Hanna Segal and Riccardo Steiner, which was published soon after Rosenfeld's death (1987), will give the reader the brief facts of his life. Here I will only mention that he was born in Nuremberg on 2 July 1910, into a middle-class Jewish family, and after studying medicine at several German universities, came to England to escape Nazi persecution in 1935. He was required to retake his medical exams which he did in Glasgow in 1936 and then, in order to acquire clinical experience with psychotic hospitalised patients, attended the Warneford Hospital near Oxford and the Maudsley Hospital in London. Later he trained as a psychotherapist at the Tavistock Clinic and then started his analysis with Klein as a candidate at the Institute of Psychoanalysis where he qualified in 1945. He then embarked on a life of extraordinary energy and creativity which involved a passionate interest in psychoanalysis until his death from a stroke in 1986.

I knew him personally, first as a student and supervisee and then as a junior colleague going for further supervision from time to time and regularly attending his post-graduate seminar. He was a tall friendly man with a warm smile but always with a serious purpose, even though expressed with a twinkle in his eye. I am a great admirer of his work and grew very fond of him but also found him frustrating and disappointing at times. He was renowned for his long sentences and for the way he repeated things over and over again, which sometimes made for hard but still worthwhile listening. I remember one occasion in supervision when I complained that he had repeated something to me four times that I had already understood the first time. He patiently repeated it again and it was only then that I realised that I had not quite understood it. On another occasion he was speaking to me about a patient of mine with an erotic transference and I again became impatient since this aspect was perfectly clear to me. He patiently explained that what I failed to understand was that the patient was not simply attracted to me but was convinced that I was attracted to her. This extra step in understanding the patient's experience is typical of Rosenfeld and takes the process to a deeper level. By recognising that projective identification may create a delusional transference in which the analyst's mind becomes the focus of the patient's attention he pointed to a feature which is of course most prominent in psychotic and borderline patients but is seen in less ill patients in a less concrete form. It marks the point where erotic transference becomes erotomania. This is also of central importance in relation to aggressive impulses which may, when projected, lead to the conviction that the patient is hated by the analyst.

In all these situations when the patient believes the analyst to be over-involved with them either in a positive or negative way, Rosenfeld recognised that projective identification plays a central role, but he never overlooked the analyst's contribution to the paranoid experience and he recognised that his own intense interest in his patients and their mental processes was sometimes felt by the patient to be intrusive. His unique capacity to put himself imaginatively into his patient's position to see things from their point of view, included their perceptions and appraisals of their analyst. Combined with this he had the equally impressive capacity to view the patient from the outside and to keep in mind the experiences of the analyst as he struggled with the patient's problems as well as his own.

In the final ten years of his life (1976–86) he became concerned that some analysts, particularly some Kleinians, interpreted in a manner which traumatised their patients. He believed that when patients had been deprived or traumatised in their childhood, they were likely to be re-traumatised in their analyses unless the analyst took special care to avoid this. In particular he believed that envy should not be too frequently interpreted and that the patient's idealisation of his analyst should not be prematurely interfered with by interpretation. Most of his writing in this late period seeks to illustrate errors that analysts can make which he believed led to an impasse in treatment, and to recommend changes which he argued could alleviate and sometimes remedy the situation. This is a difficult area to evaluate because it is only too clear that we are none of us beyond criticism and many of the points Rosenfeld makes in his late work are not only valid but represent important issues which we sometimes neglect to our cost. I will try to explain later why I believe that the shift was nevertheless away from the fine sensitivity of his classic period which I value so highly.

DEPERSONALISATION AND TRANSFERENCE PSYCHOSIS: MILDRED (1947)

Rosenfeld was an enthusiastic follower of Melanie Klein, and it is evident, particularly in his early papers, how much he admired her approach to psychoanalysis. He qualified in 1945 but continued his personal analysis during the period for some time after this and was particularly influenced by her work on splitting and projection which he learned about through his own analysis as well as from her paper of 1946 (Grosskurth 1989). His contribution was certainly very much indebted to the ideas she put forward in that paper but was also highly original and innovative.

The case of Mildred (Chapter 7, this volume) helped Rosenfeld to initiate his thinking in many of the areas in which he was to make important contributions in the future, as well as some which others were to go on and develop. For example, he described the schizoid mechanisms of ego fragmentation which lay behind depersonalisation, and this was an idea which was taken up later by Bion (1956, 1962) in his study of pathological splitting. Projective identification was, of course, a central theme and in this early paper was specifically elaborated in connection with the patient's fear of being intruded on by the analyst. For a time Mildred was even afraid she would begin to speak in a foreign accent like Rosenfeld's, and the fear of being taken over and the paranoid ideation associated with it was seen as central to the psychotic transference and the impasse which resulted from it.

Rosenfeld suggested that a delusional state developed which arose in part from the projection of the patient's own intrusiveness and he described the role played by greed and envy which he believed contributed to it. This paper also includes detailed descriptions of the clinical situation which led to his ideas on narcissism and narcissistic organisations that were to be developed further in later papers.

The title of this paper 'Analysis of a schizophrenic state with depersonalisation', is perhaps misleading because Mildred was not really schizophrenic, although psychotic mechanisms were involved in the development of a psychotic transference. Problems developed in her analysis and for a period she took to her bed and expected her mother to care for her so that she missed sessions and came forty minutes late for weeks on end. The depersonalisation was manifest by her complaints of feeling dead and cut off, with a lack of emotion, as if there was something like a blanket separating her from the world. This was associated with sensations of fragmentation which Rosenfeld believed were more prominent after a good experience and led to feelings of envy and frustration. There was widespread splitting and projection of parts of herself into her friends and family as well as into the analyst. He wrote, "It seemed as if all thought-processes, actions, and impulses, were split into innumerable parts, isolated from one another and kept in a state of division" (1947: 136 and pp. 98–9 this volume). This was a point taken up later by Bion (1962) in his discussion of pathological splitting.

From childhood Mildred had a fantasy that there was a devil who attacked what she called the good people and was keeping them tied up in dungeons. No sooner did they manage to get free then the devil appeared, attacked them violently, and tied them up even more tightly than before. Readers will recognise how similar this is to the internal structure of a narcissistic organisation which Rosenfeld was to describe in 1971a.

Mildred's experience of her analyst as persecuting and intrusive dominated the sessions but gradually one could discern the emergence of depressive anxieties and she became sad and afraid that if she began to cry that she would not be able to stop. She remembered that in the land army she was mainly afraid that she would not get up in the morning to milk the cows, forgetting them for days. This led to the fear that the good and nourishing milk was wasted and pain was inflicted on the animals. Rosenfeld linked this to her fear that missing sessions made her feel she had attacked the breast by refusing to take the milk. This mixture of depressive and paranoid anxieties was to be studied further in his paper on superego conflict in 1952 (Rosenfeld 1952a).

HOMOSEXUALITY AS A DEFENCE AGAINST PARANOIA (1949)

Following his experience with Mildred, Rosenfeld became interested in the basic pattern of transference psychosis in which the intrusive projection of impulses into the analyst led to paranoid fears and, in his next paper (1949), he studied these mechanisms in three homosexual patients. Contrary to Freud (1911), who saw the paranoia as secondary to homosexuality, Rosenfeld found that the reverse was true and that his patient's homosexuality seemed to be a defence against paranoia.

The third patient described in this paper developed an acute psychosis when he had to go into hospital with an attack of pleurisy. He was convinced he was going to die and believed that the doctors and nurses were in league against him to deceive him about this fact. Later in the treatment the patient brought material concerned with his fear of being homosexually attacked by the analyst and of being driven mad by him. Rosenfeld recognised the complex and subtle interactions between the analyst's way of working and the patient's perceptions of him which were partly coloured by projections. When the patient had a dream in which a German professor on a motor bicycle tried to split himself in two by running against a gatepost, he seemed to be expressing his view that the analyst also used splitting as a mental mechanism.

This patient also described a dream which seems to me to be a classic representation of a transference psychosis. In this dream he saw a famous surgeon operating on a patient, and he observed with great admiration the skill displayed by the surgeon, who seemed intensely concentrated on his work. Suddenly the surgeon lost his balance and fell right into the inside of the patient, with whom he got so entangled that he could scarcely manage to free himself. He nearly choked and only by administering an oxygen apparatus could he mange to revive himself. With this dream the patient expressed his extreme fear of the analyst getting so interested in him that he would get inside him. This dream seems to me to illustrate how Rosenfeld was able to analyse the patient's paranoia, partly as an expression of his anxiety about the intensity of Rosenfeld's interest in him, but also partly resulting from a projection of his own voyeuristic and intrusive interest in the analyst.

CONFUSIONAL STATES (1950)

In this important and original paper, Rosenfeld describes the confusion which can arise between good and bad objects and between good and bad parts of the self when normal splitting has broken down, and he argues that this confusion is very difficult for the patient to bear. Later Rosenfeld discusses a second type of confusion which results from excessive projective identification and involves confusion between what belongs to the self and what belongs to objects. This second type of confusion is not usually experienced as such by the patient, although it is often very obvious to the observing analyst. Indeed projective identification is often deployed to reduce confusion and create a sense of order to help the subject escape from an unbearable chaotic experience.

The clinical material for this paper comes from a very disturbed schizo-phrenic artist who suffered a breakdown after three months of analysis with a colleague of Rosenfeld. He became promiscuous, wore make up and behaved as if he was a homosexual prostitute, all of which seemed to be a reaction to a state of extreme confusion. This patient blamed his first analyst for confusing him by interpreting that his paintings were dark because of his wish to smear faeces. In response to this the patient stopped painting altogether until Rosenfeld saw that he also had a concept of good faeces associated with gardening and manure. He helped him to lessen the confusion by re-establishing the split between good and bad. Rosenfeld recognised that in a sense this was a retrograde step since development and integration depended on a lessening of splitting but he argued that the urgent need was to help the patient cope with the acute confusional state.

Melanie Klein later (1957) acknowledged his contribution and discussed this type of confusion in relation to envy which she saw to be responsible for the breakdown of splitting. Normal splitting enables destructive impulses to be directed to bad objects and good impulses to good objects. This may be a distortion of reality and a denial of ambivalence but at least order is maintained and Klein argued that such order was necessary to give time for the good object to be firmly established before integration can lead to the mitigation of hatred by love in the depressive position. If envy predominates, however, destructive attacks are mounted against good objects rather than bad ones in a kind of crossover of the split, and to defend against these attacks the good object is often idealised so that the split is increased. Klein described how the idealised object can itself provoke even more envious attacks, leading to even more extreme idealisation, until eventually splitting breaks down and gives rise to the confusional state. Rosenfeld was impressed with the depth of Klein's analysis and, interviewed by Grosskurth (1989: 28), expressed his regret that he had not taken his own analysis of confusional states further.

SUPEREGO CONFLICT IN AN ACUTE SCHIZOPHRENIC PATIENT (1952A)

Inspired by Klein's work on child analysis, several analysts most notably Segal (1950) and Bion (1956) joined Rosenfeld and with great courage and a pioneering spirit began to treat schizophrenic patients without abandoning the basic technique of psychoanalysis. The patient he described in this paper was a severely ill 21-year-old man in an acute psychotic breakdown who was withdrawn, hallucinated, and often mute. He made apparently meaningless utterances and was impulsively violent, sometimes needing two private nurses. Rosenfeld saw the patient six times a week for 1 hr 20 minute sessions mostly at the private clinic where he was an inpatient. Even though the analysis only lasted three months because his parents withdrew the patient from the analysis, Rosenfeld describes the treatment in great detail and is able to find meaning in material which was chaotic and fragmented.

Despite the fragmentation and the predominantly paranoid ideation the patient was also concerned with guilt particularly after he had assaulted one of the nurses. Rosenfeld saw the problem in terms of the patient's relationship with a primitive and very severe superego. Although the superego was predominantly persecutory in this patient, he recognised a more complex picture which also included a relationship with a helpful superego towards which the patient felt depressive guilt of an extreme severity. Both the persecutory and helpful superego figures emerged in the transference and could be analysed as the transference was analysed just as it would be with an ordinary non-psychotic patient. The main differences in technique which the patient's illness demanded involved the sort of adjustments that an analyst often has to make in the analysis of children. The parents and nurses had to be spoken to and the material itself was observed and interpreted rather in the way Klein did in her play technique.

In a further paper on the same patient (1952b) Rosenfeld presented additional clinical material and argued that it was possible to analyse the transference even in patients as regressed and hallucinated as this patient was. Both the positive and negative transference were observed and led to a painful superego conflict between persecutory and helpful internal objects.

Rosenfeld quickly became one of the leading proponents of the psycho-analytic treatment of psychotic patients, especially of schizophrenia, and wrote many accounts and reviews of his work and that of others (1954, 1963, 1964a, 1964b, 1969, 1981, 1987). These will not be discussed separately here but the reader can refer to the detailed survey of this work in the appendix of *Impasse and Interpretation* (Rosenfeld 1987: 281).

THE PSYCHOPATHOLOGY OF NARCISSISM (1964c)

Rosenfeld's papers on narcissism are to my mind his most important contribution to psychoanalysis. In the first of these (Chapter 8, this volume), he spells out what constitutes narcissism, describes the mental mechanisms which lead to its establishment and details the defensive purpose which narcissism serves.

His first point, which he reiterated many times in later papers, is that Freud was wrong to suggest that narcissistic patients do not establish a transference relationship. Instead he argues that narcissism is a form of primitive object relationship that is sometimes so successfully disguised that it masquerades as a state of withdrawal in which no object relationships are apparent. The presenting symptoms and personality of narcissistic patients can vary greatly but Rosenfeld described a basic pattern in all of these patients in which the appropriation of admirable qualities belonging to the object is followed by an admiration and overvaluation of the self.

The mechanisms leading to this type of object relationship are spelled out in detail and illustrated in the case material. They are based on omnipotent identifications through which desirable aspects of the object are possessed and undesirable ones are disowned. Rosenfeld speaks of the object, usually a part object – the breast – which is omnipotently incorporated and treated as the infant's possession while at the same time the mother or breast are used as containers into which parts of the self, which are felt to be undesirable as they cause pain or anxiety, are omnipotently projected. Sometimes the desired qualities are acquired by introjection but Rosenfeld also describes projective identification being used omnipotently to enter an object to take over qualities which would be experienced as desirable. The narcissistic patient can then claim either to be the desired object, or to possess the desired qualities (1964c: 170–1 and p. 107 this volume).

The projection of undesirable qualities into the analyst may lead to him being treated, and sometimes portrayed in dreams, as a lavatory or lap so that any disturbing feeling or sensation can be immediately evacuated. Even though the object is devalued, the situation is felt to be ideal since all discomfort is immediately got rid of. This is a familiar experience for many analysts who recognise how some patients assume that this is part of the analyst's contractual duty and feel betrayed if it is called into question.

A central theme developed in this paper is that the narcissistic relationship is a defence against separateness. When the object is omnipotently possessed the self becomes so identified with it that all separate identity or boundary between self and object is lost. This means that the subject treats the object as if he were a part of himself and not a separate person with his own characteristics. He may ignore aspects of the object which do not fit the projection or he may control and force or persuade the object to enact the role required of him.

Rosenfeld follows Klein (1957) and Abraham (1924) in suggesting that defences against envy play a central role in narcissistic relationships. Separateness, dependence and envy all go together and the omnipotent narcissistic object relationship which prevents awareness of separateness, obviates both the aggressive feelings caused by frustration and destructive ones provoked by envy. When the infant omnipotently possesses the mother's breast, the breast cannot frustrate him or arouse his envy. Rosenfeld argued that envy which is felt to be unbearable increases the difficulty of tolerating dependence and frustration (1964c: 171 and p. 108 this volume).

I find it surprising that Rosenfeld does not mention that narcissistic defences protect the patient from experience of loss. Perhaps he was dealing with psychotic patients operating at a paranoid–schizoid level but even in these patients he was aware of depressive feelings and described a depressive superego (1952a). A recognition that the object is separate from the self means that it is capable of being lost, a relationship which Freud himself was aware of in the distinction he made between an anaclitic and a narcissistic object choice. He is particularly clear in the famous tiny fragment found posthumously, entitled "Having" and "being" in children. Here he writes,

> Children like expressing an object relation by an identification: "I am the object". "Having" is the later of the two; after the loss of the object

> it relapses into "being". Example: the breast. "The breast is a part of me, I am the breast". Only later "I have it" that is "I am not it". . . .
>
> (Freud 1941: 299–300)

I think he also implies that, if I am the breast I cannot lose the breast, it is part of me! But Freud also writes that after the loss of the object the anaclitic relationship with a separate object relapses into an identification, and the pain of loss is avoided.

Later Rosenfeld designated the type of narcissism described in this paper as libidinal narcissism, because it is based on idealisation and possession of good elements in the patient and in his objects. He contrasts it with destructive narcissism, which is more violent but he makes it clear that even in this libidinal form very powerful destructive forces and phantasies are evoked if the narcissism is challenged. Moreover he argued that even though the discovery of the patient's dependence on his objects may temporarily lead to him feeling severely deflated, it is essential for this theme to be faced and understood if real relations are ever to be established. Later in his work on destructive narcissism he described even more violent reactions to the experience of separateness when feelings of deflation were felt as a severe humiliation.

DESTRUCTIVE NARCISSISM (1971a)

Rosenfeld's second paper on narcissism is entitled "A clinical approach to the psychoanalytic theory of the life and death instincts: an investigation into the aggressive aspects of narcissism" (Chapter 9, this volume) and followed the first after a gap of seven years. Here he shows that, in addition to the idealisation of good elements in the self and in the object, the narcissistic patient can idealise destructive elements which are turned to as a source of strength and superiority. Rosenfeld also describes how these elements are organised into complex structures, often represented as a gang or mafia which become very resistant to change.

The introduction to this paper presents a rather complex discussion of the life and death instincts, which to the modern reader may sound a little dated. It does however draw attention to states of withdrawal commonly seen in narcissistic patients in which death is idealised as superior to life. Sometimes this takes the form of an identification with a loved dead object which the patient is reluctant to relinquish. Klein herself did not write a great deal about narcissism but she did discuss it as a state of withdrawal to an identification with an internalised ideal object (Klein 1952). In this paper Rosenfeld suggests a similar withdrawal but to an idealised destructive object which pulls or seduces the good parts of the self towards death and destructiveness. Indeed he suggests that this type of withdrawal is close to an expression of an un-fused death instinct pulling the patient towards death. However, he is always aware of a remnant of life instinct which he tries to make contact with and through which it is sometimes possible to rescue the patient.

Rosenfeld makes an important distinction between normal fusion of instincts and pathological fusion. While normal fusion, like the integration of good and bad parts of the self, can lead to a modification and amelioration of destructiveness by bringing it in contact with loving feelings, he was struck by the fact that this is not true when destructive phantasies become erotised. Fusion with life instinct in that case actually increases the cruelty and destructiveness in the form of sadism and he thought of this as a pathological fusion of the instincts.

I think we mostly prefer to think of these issues in terms of the idealisation of destructive objects and destructive parts of the self which was the theme he was to develop in the later sections of the paper. However, the idea of the death instinct has another important connection in relation to envy which Klein, and of course Rosenfeld also, considered to be its chief representation. Narcissistic object relationships which nullify experience of separateness protect the patient from any awareness of difference, and it is precisely the existence of difference which stimulates envy. Indeed the connection of envy to the death instinct is most clear when we recognise that the aim of envious attacks is to destroy difference by reducing both subject and object to a deadly nothingness. If everything is reduced to dust there is no envy as there is nothing to be envious of. For some patients it is only then that a peaceful existence can be imagined. Feldman (2000) has suggested that envy can be more appropriately thought of as an anti-life instinct rather than as an instinct seeking death and this remains a controversial question. To my mind the vital issue discussed here has to do with the acknowledgement and responsibility for envy and for the type of destructiveness based on envy. This has to be differentiated from aggression in the service of the life instinct, such as is seen in protecting good objects and also in pursuing normal healthy rivalries and jealousies. Abraham (1919), Klein (1957), and now Rosenfeld emphasise that split off and unacknowledged envy is a particular feature of narcissistic states and gives rise to profound obstacles to development and prevents psychic change. Not much can be done to moderate the destructive effects of envy unless it can be reintegrated and come into conjunction with reparative and constructive parts of the personality. It is this modification of envy by love and gratitude which Rosenfeld thought of in terms of a beneficial fusion of the life and death instincts.

Rosenfeld goes on then to consider narcissistic object relations clinically and begins with a summary of his description of libidinal narcissism in his 1964 paper (Rosenfeld 1964c). In the case of destructive narcissism, self-idealisation also plays a central role, but now involves an idealisation of destructive parts of the self and destructive objects. The destructiveness is directed both against any positive libidinal object relationship and any libidinal part of the self which experiences need for an object and the desire to depend on it. The destructiveness often remains disguised or split off but in fact has a very powerful effect in preventing dependent object relations and in keeping external objects permanently devalued, which accounts for the apparent indifference of the narcissistic individual towards external objects and the world.

When libidinal aspects predominate contact with an object which is perceived as separate from the self often leads the patient to feel deflated and defeated by the revelation that it is the external object which, in reality, contains the valuable qualities which he had attributed to his own creative powers. However, when destructive aspects predominate the humiliation is more extreme and envy is manifest as a violent wish to destroy the analyst when he represents the source of life and goodness.

Rosenfeld describes how self-destructive impulses may draw the patient into an alliance with death and a hatred of all elements in the personality which seek life and liveliness. Here his descriptions are vivid and memorable, perhaps particularly in his account of the narcissistic gang (1971a: 174 and p. 125 this volume).

Rosenfeld also describes perverse aspects of narcissism in which erotisation increases the sadism of the organisation and also psychotic versions in which the patient is drawn into a delusional world, that often promises omnipotent solutions to his desperate situation. He argues that it is essential to help the patient to find and rescue the dependent sane part of the self from its trapped position inside the psychotic narcissistic structure and to help him to become fully conscious of the split-off destructive omnipotent parts of the self.

I find his clinical descriptions quite moving, particularly the one of a patient who dreamt of a small boy who was in a comatose condition, lying exposed in the hot sun. The patient was standing nearby but did nothing, only feeling critical and superior to the doctor who should have seen that the child was moved into the shade. It seemed to illustrate a common experience where the patient keeps himself disabled and refuses to help or to be helped, while blaming others for the neglect.

I have personally been particularly influenced by this paper and have discussed Rosenfeld's narcissistic organisations in terms of psychic retreats and pathological organisation of the personality (Steiner 1993). Despite the controversies which surround theories of the life and death instinct I find the discussion of fusion and defusion of instincts to be important particularly because of its relevance to the basic problem all patients have in the integration of destructiveness into the personality, especially when the destructiveness is based on envy. I believe many of the defensive manoeuvres that Rosenfeld describes are attempts to neutralise and bind destructiveness, which may serve temporarily to relieve the patient but which gives rise to prolonged and deep resistances to development.

PROJECTIVE IDENTIFICATION (1971b)

This paper (Chapter 10, this volume) was given in Canada at a symposium on problems of psychosis and remained tucked away in a little known collection from this conference (Rosenfeld 1971b) until it was reprinted by Elisabeth Bott Spillius in her volume entitled *Melanie Klein Today* (1988). Although the paper emphasises the situation in psychotic patients most of the detailed discussion of projective identification is applicable with little modification to other patients as well.

Rosenfeld's summary of Klein's contribution, particularly that put forward in her paper on schizoid mechanisms (1946) is especially clear in this paper which makes it a good introduction to the subject in general. He emphasises a basic pattern in which projective identification gives rise to paranoid anxieties and seriously interferes with introjection because the patient fears a forceful entry from the outside in retribution for violent projections. Here we have Klein's work providing an understanding of some of the basic mechanisms which underlie Rosenfeld's findings on the psychotic transference and on the impasse which results. It seems clear that he took his basic orientation from Klein but was able to expound his own views which extended her ideas and which also provided descriptions of the clinical situation where her views could be applied.

Rosenfeld then develops his view that several different types of projective identification and several different motives for using it can be discerned and differentiated. First he distinguishes projective identification used for communication from projective identification used to unburden the psyche of unwanted parts. He recognises that both may be operating simultaneously but he sees it as important to distinguish the two. If he is trying to communicate the patient wants the analyst to understand, while if he is trying to evacuate he wants the analyst to sanction the evacuation, and interpretations may then be seen as a counter-projection on the part of the analyst. Of course the different motives interact and it is often precisely when the patient is violently evacuating that he most needs to be contained and understood. Rosenfeld's ideas on the communicative aspects of projective identification are very similar to those found in the work of Bion on containment (1962), and both men were concerned to understand the fate of elements in the personality which could not be tolerated by the patient. Rosenfeld was often to stress that what was projected was not only internal objects but also parts of the self and that containment can only be helpful if the analyst can relate to the communicative element in the projection and can transform these into a form that the patient can accept as helpful. Even though, for my part, Rosenfeld becomes a bit didactic and classificatory, I find myself impressed by his capacity to tune into the patient's need to be understood even if the patient seems more obviously to be intent on evacuation or attack.

A further type of projective identification described in this paper might be referred to as possessive projective identification, and involves the aim of controlling the analyst's body and mind, and often involves a phantasy that the patient has omnipotently forced himself into the analyst and taken over his functions. Sometimes, when mad parts of the self are projected, the analyst is perceived as mad, and the patient is afraid the interpretations will drive him mad in turn. This was part of the transference psychosis in Rosenfeld's original description of Mildred's analysis.

The fusion or confusion with the analyst has many consequences and is of course an essential feature of the narcissistic type of object relationship in which the analyst's qualities are taken over, identified with and idealised. In this paper Rosenfeld emphasises problems that arise because of the concrete thinking, which is another consequence of the lack of distinction between self and object. He quotes Segal (1950), who made the important distinction between symbol and symbolic equivalent, and reminds us how important it is to recognise that the patient may experience the interpretation as a concrete thing which he feels is being forced into him.

Throughout his work on narcissism and on projective identification Rosenfeld has repeatedly stressed the role of envy and, in particular, the way projective identification is used to avoid experience of envy by a taking over and possession of the good qualities of the object. This may mean however that the patient feels himself to be the target of envious attacks by others, as he now contains all the goodness and his own envy is projected. When the patient begins to feel more separate and relates to the analyst more as a separate person, violent destructive impulses make their appearance which often have an envious quality. When this happened Rosenfeld's patients sometimes reacted with feelings of humiliation and complained of being made to feel small when the analyst reminded him of depending on something he needed but which he could not provide for himself. Influenced by him I have argued that it is easy to inflict humiliations on our patients and then to fail to recognise the cause of their sensitivity and distress (Steiner 2003, 2006).

Finally Rosenfeld discusses two more pathological forms of projective identification which involve a phantasy of living right inside the analyst. In the delusional form the patient seems to enter a mad world where he believes there is complete painlessness and freedom to indulge in any whim. Used in this way the delusional object exerts a powerful suggestive and seductive influence on saner parts of the personality in an attempt to persuade or force them to withdraw from reality and to join the delusional omnipotent world. He also describes a form of projective identification in which the patient behaves like a parasite, living on the capabilities of the analyst who is expected to function as his ego. This parasitic state can be extremely chronic and progress may be minimal, as the patient becomes passive, silent and sluggish, demanding everything and giving nothing in return.

These situations which involve the use of projective identification to intrude into the analyst seem different from those in which an unwanted part of the self is split off and attributed to the object. The identity of the self seems to be lost and the patient may either assume a borrowed identity or if some sense of self is retained he may feel trapped inside an object and be unable to extricate himself. These reactions are more often seen in those psychotic patients who assume the identity of another person, say Napoleon, but they are also probably related to those patients who live a vicarious existence using someone else to gain an identity from. This is one form of "as-if" patient and was described by Klein in her paper "On Identification" (1955).

Rosenfeld is always concerned to link theory with technique and in this paper discusses special treatment needs of the psychotic patient. He emphasises the importance of recognising the existence of a sane part of the patient who wants to use the analysis and is constantly threatened by an omnipotent part of the self. The interesting patient Rosenfeld describes in this paper had a schizophrenic breakdown some years previously but was now no longer deluded or hallucinated. However, he continued to feel drawn into a mad world with fears of loss of identity and a feeling of being trapped. When Rosenfeld took an unusually timed break of two weeks in the autumn the patient became very disturbed and described feeling that he could not drag himself away from the TV screen as he watched the Olympic Games taking place in Mexico. He felt forced to watch and complained that he was being drawn into the hot climate of Mexico which made him feel unwell. At times he felt so strongly pulled into the TV that he felt claustrophobic and had difficulty breathing.

Despite some paranoid anxieties the patient improved and depressive aspects began to emerge. Again he had a dream that he was watching Olympic runners on television, but this time he was not drawn to compete but instead he got angry when he saw a number of people crowding the track and interfering with the race. Rosenfeld interpreted that the people represented parts of himself wanting to greedily and enviously enter and interfere with the running. He thought he was also enviously attacking the analyst when he felt admiration and envy for him just as he had for the athletes. The patient, however, was now not completely identified with the intruding elements and wanted to stop them invading.

Many other aspects of this patient's treatment were described but I wanted to highlight the intrusiveness as an important theme which recurs in Rosenfeld's work, and is the focus of the paper by O'Shaughnessy in Chapter 1 of the present volume. The patient's intrusiveness so clearly described in the dream did not nevertheless seem to the patient to originate from within. Rather he felt pulled into the TV set by a force outside him and this is often how a psychotic process is experienced. I see it as similar to the dream Rosenfeld described in the paper on homosexuality which I discussed earlier (1949) except that in that dream it was the analyst who was felt to be so interested in his patient that he was represented as a surgeon who was pulled into the abdomen of the patient he was operating on.

PAPERS ON STRACHEY'S MUTATIVE INTERPRETATIONS (1972), AND ON NEGATIVE THERAPEUTIC REACTIONS (1975)

These two papers take the form of reviews rather than original contributions and show Rosenfeld's appreciation of the work of other analysts. In his discussion of Strachey's paper for example he emphasised his basic agreement with this now classic view of the importance of the analysis of transference in which the analyst appears as a superego figure. However, he added to this formulation by suggesting that it was not only internal objects which were projected onto the analyst but split-off parts of the ego as well, so that the analyst came to function as an auxiliary ego as well as an auxiliary superego.

His paper on negative therapeutic reactions (1975) includes a detailed and illuminating review of both Karen Horney's (1936), and Joan Riviére's (1936), contribution to this subject. While the importance of split-off envy and the role of narcissistic object relations remain central to Rosenfeld's approach he is clearly impressed and touched by Riviére's description of the patient's experience of unconscious guilt and despair when faced with the state of his internal objects. Rosenfeld appreciates the depth and sensitivity which she shows in her attention to depressive features and while these have always been part of his overall clinical approach they have perhaps had less prominence in his theoretical writing because of his preoccupation with schizoid patients and schizoid mechanisms. Riviére argued that not all negative therapeutic reactions should be seen as attempts to defeat the analysis, since the patient may have a prior obligation to rescue damaged internal objects which may take precedence over his ability to accept help for himself. This is a theme developed further by Henri Rey (1988), who was analysed by Rosenfeld and supervised by Riviére in his paper on "That which Patients Bring to Analysis".

Rosenfeld was able to use his understanding of Klein's work on schizoid mechanisms and in particular her descriptions of primitive envy to integrate this with his awareness of the patient's depressive feelings. What was most impressive to me was Rosenfeld's ability to present a balanced view and to understand that as the patient came to recognise his destructiveness it also evoked the pain and guilt which was based on his love and concern for his objects. When this guilt and pain was unbearable a return to schizoid mechanisms and a narcissistic organisation provided a way out.

ROSENFELD'S PAPER IN THE BION MEMORIAL VOLUME (1981)

This paper entitled "On the Psychopathology and Treatment of Psychotic Patients, (Historical and Comparative Reflections)" appeared in the memorial volume to Bion edited by James Grotstein and in it Rosenfeld acknowledges the importance of Wilfred Bion and Hanna Segal, the two analysts contemporary with him who influenced and helped him most.

He reviews Segal's work on concrete thinking and symbolic equations and recognises that an important factor underlying transference psychosis and impasse is the concrete thinking which arises when symbolic function fails. The transference situation then becomes distorted and the interpretations are experienced as advice, criticism or seduction, rather than as ideas for the patient to consider. Bion's formulation on the patient's intolerance of verbal thought is used by Rosenfeld to argue that it is verbal thought which puts the patient in touch with his sanity and through this with an experience of psychic pain. This is close to his own view that destructive narcissism is mobilised against a sane part of the patient who wants to make contact with the analyst as a helpful figure. It is also clear that the idea of a destructive part of the personality is central to Rosenfeld's work and is influenced by Bion's discussion of the differentiation of psychotic and non-psychotic parts of the personality (Bion 1957).

The clinical material Rosenfeld uses in this paper to illustrate transference and counter-transference interaction is taken from a schizophrenic patient of my own whose analysis Rosenfeld supervised for a time. With this patient I found I had to resist an intense desire to sleep, and I found Rosenfeld very helpful in my struggle with this reaction. In this paper he describes a dream my patient reported in which he was walking on a meadow and thinking of lying down when he noticed that the meadow was covered by thousands of bees. He then explained that he feared he was being lulled into a false complacency. Rosenfeld helped me to connect the dream and the complacency with my own reaction and I was able to observe myself being persuaded by the patient that everything was going well and there was nothing to worry about. I felt myself pulled into a hypnotic state by the patient's material which I was sometimes unable to resist. I remember being impressed when Rosenfeld linked this to the patient's struggle with the omnipotent psychotic force and also to the Bzzz Bzzz of the bees in the dream which was lulling me to sleep.

At the end of this paper in the Bion memorial volume Rosenfeld makes some important comments on the oft-quoted injunction Bion gave to avoid "memory and desire". While he agrees on the importance of keeping an open mind, Rosenfeld argues that it is impossible for the analyst to destroy desire and intention, because he is human, and he cannot avoid wanting things for his patient and for himself. Moreover, if the analyst tries to eliminate rather than to understand his memories and desires he is in danger of dehumanising himself and severely damaging the relationship with the patient.

THE FINAL PHASE OF ROSENFELD'S ANALYTIC APPROACH, 1978–1987

Beginning with his paper on "Some Therapeutic Factors in Psychoanalysis" (1978a), I believe we can see a change in Rosenfeld's clinical and theoretical approach which reaches its clearest exposition in *Impasse and Interpretation* (1987). I will try and describe how these changes emerge in his writings in this final ten-year period and discuss them further in relation to his 1987 book.

The paper on therapeutic factors (1978a), in my view, is really about anti-therapeutic factors on the part of the analyst, and Rosenfeld thought that many of these arose from the analyst's failure to adopt the right attitude to his patients. In particular he stressed that the patient's criticisms of the analyst should not necessarily be treated as attacks but listened to seriously as communications about the analyst's work. In principle this is not a contentious point and most analysts would agree that the patient is often able to pick up important errors in the analyst's work, as well as in his attitude, as it is reflected in his general approach as well as in his inter-pretations. The patient will attempt to convey to the analyst how his work is being received, and often something like a helpful supervision can emerge, provided that the analyst is able to accept criticism. However Rosenfeld seemed to me to adopt the patient's criticisms too simply as a correct description of the analyst rather than as his subjective experience which had to be balanced by other observations. His approach presents a problem to those analysts who argue that it is common for the patient's statements to be multi-determined and that attacks are often mounted against the analytic work and the analytic setting, while at the same time the criticisms may be valid to various degrees.

Rosenfeld's example is from a young analyst who persisted in inter-preting the patient's anger about a weekend and failed to pick up that the patient felt the problem lay in the analyst's unwillingness to listen to him in the sessions. The patient then complained that the analyst delayed opening the door to let him into the consulting room because he did not hear the buzzer. Rosenfeld was able to recognise that the patient was commenting on the more general unavailability of the analyst during sessions and had in mind particular occasions when he felt that the analyst was preoccupied with his own needs and was not sufficiently responsive to those of his patient. In a second example a patient's dreams involved scenes of punish-ment, persecution and blame, and Rosenfeld felt that this communicated the patient's view that the analyst's interpretations had been accusing and guilt-provoking.

This attention to the patient's communication has become an accepted part of the analytic attitude and I think we owe a debt to Rosenfeld for drawing our attention to the way even disturbed patients can make accurate and insightful observations about the analyst's attitude and behaviour. Certainly I was influenced by him to listen to the patient in this way and I often feel that a shift occurs if I can take the patient's comments and criticisms as an accurate reflection of my work. However, to my mind, Rosenfeld increasingly seemed to find fault with the analyst's work and was less inclined to explore the complex interactions between factors in the patient and those in the analyst.

This contrasts with the fine sensitivity he previously showed, when he seemed to be able to put himself into the patient's position with great delicacy but also to withdraw, to observe what was going on in himself and between himself and the patient. For example, I have discussed earlier Rosenfeld's description of the patient who dreamed that Rosenfeld was a surgeon who fell into the abdomen of his patient during an operation. Here he interpreted that the patient saw him as too interested in his work, and while he recognised that it was in some ways an accurate description of himself, he also linked it with the patient's own tendency to intrude into the analyst.

These new technical developments were associated with a new theory to which Rosenfeld gave more and more emphasis and he came to believe that many of these patients had suffered early infantile trauma and deprivation and that the analyst's work was experienced as further trauma when the patients came to treatment. These patients were later described as thin skinned (see Chapter 13 of *Impasse and Interpretation*, p. 274) and Rosenfeld believed that the repetition of the trauma could be prevented if the analyst recognised the patient's vulnerability and avoided interpretations which could repeat this trauma. He argued that it was therefore important not to interpret aggression or narcissism but rather to absorb and contain the attacks which he held were both necessary and to have a primary communicative function. In my view this leads to a confusion between how the analyst is perceived by the patient and how he actually is, a distinction which is often very crucial and very difficult to determine, and about which most analysts believe it is vital to keep an open mind, exploring both possibilities in as even handed a manner as possible. Rosenfeld's approach as described now is also very different from his earlier style which involved a sensitivity to the patient's pain accompanied by a recognition that the patient cannot always be protected from painful experiences. It of course involves a distinction between preventable and unnecessary suffering and that which is an integral part of engaging in life and in relationships. Writing in 1964 about the pain of having the patient's dependence on his object recognised, Rosenfeld argues that,

The unmasking of the situation, while it may temporarily lead to the patient's feeling severely deflated, is essential if real relations to external and internal objects are ever to be established.

(1964c: 176 and p. 111 this volume)

PAPERS ON BORDERLINE PATIENTS (1978b, 1979)

Another shift in Rosenfeld's attitude begins to emerge in his papers on borderline patients where I think he comes to be interested in diagnostic distinctions much more than he had previously. Before the late 1970s he had been interested in mechanisms and in the way defences were organised and he recognised narcissistic object relations to exist in a wide range of patients. It is true that he spoke about borderline psychotic patients and that he did differentiate between libidinal and destructive narcissism, but with the 1978 paper he took the process further and he began to differentiate between different types of borderline patients. Here I think one can see the influence of Kernberg (1975) who strongly supported the idea of careful diagnosis of the pathology of the patient and then of tailoring the treatment appropriate to each type of patient. Indeed Rosenfeld singles out the writing of Kernberg on borderline personality organisations in his review and finds himself in agreement with many of his ideas.

His own interest in this paper is in the severely traumatised borderline patient and he argues that a change in analytic technique is required to avoid or to overcome the transference psychosis which is likely to develop at some point in the analysis of these patients. He believes they have suffered painful deprivations which caused long-lasting experiences of rage and anxiety particularly connected with a fear of death. Moreover these anxieties have not been relieved by a containing environment because the mother was sometimes absent but more often present but unable to cope because of her own preoccupations and anxieties. The patient as a child may then have become convinced that his normal liveliness is something bad, and wrongly described as destructiveness and aggression. Rosenfeld describes the patient's painful experience of being attacked and made to feel all bad by a terribly severe superego, against which he may defend himself by withdrawal or by himself violently attacking the analyst, when he feels that the analyst is not able to contain and understand his projections. Rosenfeld argues that this situation requires a different technical approach from that which he advocated earlier, and in particular that interpretations of destructiveness and envy should be avoided.

To illustrate his approach Rosenfeld described a patient who had early feeding difficulties and long separations from his mother. After about two and a half years of treatment he became increasingly hostile and critical, not only of what the analyst said but of his tone and body movements, making

Rosenfeld feel like "a small child battered into a helpless rage by his relentless accusations". Eventually the patient decided to break off his analysis and Rosenfeld asked the patient to sit up, and encouraged him to go over the criticisms which he listened to without giving any interpretations but adopting instead a receptive empathic listening attitude. Rosenfeld believed that it was this which enabled the patient to continue his treatment for a while and he argued that the result supported Kernberg's idea that some transference situations cannot be analysed without changes in analytic technique. Previously Rosenfeld had set great store on retaining an analytic attitude even in the face of transference psychosis and this approach seems to represent a change in his technique and in his attitude. I have found that the patient often becomes extremely anxious if the analyst makes such departures from his usual analytic approach and he may come to believe that the analyst has given up on him and has lost confidence in the analytic method. Of course in rare cases an impasse becomes so deep that the analysis may not be able to continue and a very difficult and painful step towards ending may need to take place.

In the second of the borderline papers (1979), classification is taken further but he did not come back to this classification again and I don't think his heart was in it. He did, however, remain convinced of important distinctions between different patients which had correspondingly important implications for technique. In particular he distinguished between patients with destructive narcissism from those with libidinal narcissism and between traumatised thin-skinned and non-traumatised thick-skinned patients.

PRIMITIVE OBJECT RELATIONS (1983)

In July 1982 Rosenfeld, together with Betty Joseph and Hanna Segal, took part in a conference celebrating the centenary of Melanie Klein's birth, organised and chaired by Ron Britton and myself. As befitted the occasion Rosenfeld reviewed Klein's contribution and in particular her work on schizoid mechanisms and projective identification which were especially important for him. In fact he began by returning to Mildred, his first training case, and once more to the theme of intrusiveness which clearly continued to occupy him. He reiterated how much he owed to Klein and to the fact that he was in analysis with her at the time he was treating Mildred, which was precisely the time she was working on schizoid mechanisms.

On this occasion he restates his earlier view that Mildred's paranoid fear of him, including the fear of being taken over by him, arose from the projection of her own intrusive wishes but he now argued that the situation was more complex than he had previously thought and that projective identification covers a broad range of rather different processes.

Rosenfeld brings some of his views on projective identification up to date and describes the various ways the patient can become entangled and confused with the analyst. As in his previous paper on projective identification (1971b), he stresses that the most important distinction is that between projective identification used for communication and that used for purposes of evacuation, destruction, or control. Communicative projective identification, he argues, is essentially benign and does not change the state of the object. In this form the projections can be received, contained, modified and then returned to the patient when they have been understood by the analyst, according to the model put forward by Bion (1962). By contrast, in evacuative projective identification the patient demands that the analyst condones the denial and if he tries to give some of the unwanted mental contents back, the patient violently resists.

Towards the end of this paper Rosenfeld begins a discussion of the problems created in patients who have been projected into during their infancy and childhood. This type of patient also tries to project violently in order to get rid of tension and pressure from inside, but because the pressure originated outside him, he feels himself to be a victim of projections, and may feel persecuted if the analyst does not recognise this fact. Again Rosenfeld seems to leave aside the need for the analyst to remain neutral and to leave open the question of where the original projection came from. Of course it goes without saying that it is vital to remember not only that the patient may have been projected into as a child but that the analyst can be induced to do the same and to re-traumatise the patient.

Rosenfeld concludes with the description of a patient of this type who felt that she had to get rid of unbearable internal pressure and confusion which left her with no space to take anything in. In the sessions she seemed to be under enormous tension and Rosenfeld thought that she was afraid that her violent intrusions into her analyst confused him and drove him mad. Eventually she was able to link this with her experience of her mother's manic breakdown which she felt as an unstoppable intrusion into herself. She also remembered her mother approaching her in a friendly way and then squeezing her boils and Rosenfeld realised that often she felt she was not herself but her mother when she intruded into him demanding help. Again Rosenfeld seems to be making a judgement about where the disturbance originated.

IMPASSE AND INTERPRETATION (1987)

Rosenfeld's last work is his book, *Impasse and Interpretation*, in which he reviews and revises his thinking on most of the important topics he tackled throughout his career as a psychoanalyst. This book is admired by many and to my mind displays those features which make his late work so controversial. Those of us who knew him at the time he was writing the book were all aware of a tremendous pressure he was under to complete this work, and in fact he died soon after it was finished and before it appeared in print. The reader will be impressed with the sheer volume and detail of the clinical material, some if it from his own patients but a good deal from material reported by supervisees and in seminars. He was able to present such detail because he meticulously tape recorded his supervisions and his seminars in order to explore and demonstrate his ideas.

In the book he restates in greater detail the conclusions he draws in the papers I have already discussed. He reviews some of his classic contributions to the understanding of narcissism and narcissistic object relations, and he deals specifically with *impasse*, discussing different types of impasse and the reasons for each. There are chapters on projective identification, on the problems of containment in borderline psychotic patients, and the specific problems found in schizophrenic patients.

Special mention should be made of his overview presented in Chapter 13 of that book which provides an interesting and useful account of the changes in Rosenfeld's thinking. These have chiefly to do with factors which exacerbate and alleviate impasse and they lead him to make a number of recommendations on technique and in particular on the attitudes which the analyst should adopt when an impasse is identified.

The chief of these can be summarised as follows. The analyst should focus less on factors in the patient and more on factors in the analyst. He should be careful not to interpret envy too freely and especially to avoid making the patient feel bad, guilty or humiliated. The analyst should pay careful attention to the patient's history and pick up situations of early trauma and deprivation so that he can avoid repeating these in the analysis. He must tolerate being idealised and he should make careful diagnostic distinctions between thin-skinned and thick-skinned narcissistic patients and between libidinal and destructive narcissism because each of these demand a particular and different technical approach. Finally, he should recognise that patients may have been projected into by disturbed parents and relatives and that the analyst is in danger of doing the same if he fails to recognise his own contribution to the difficulties of the analysis.

These points all seem to me to be important and valid as *a part* of the analyst's approach provided they are balanced by the need to help the patient to face his own problems and what he brings to the situation. One of Rosenfeld's important contributions was to show how an analysis can flounder if a psychotic process leads to a delusional transference. It was always understood that the analyst can exacerbate feelings of persecution by misunderstanding the patient, but many other factors were emphasised in his early work, particularly the patient's propensity to use projective identification to control the analyst and to rid himself of undesired qualities. Now Rosenfeld sees misunderstandings on the part of the analyst to be by far the most important among the factors leading to impasse. In my view his descriptions of factors in the analyst are, in themselves, valid and important and they have helped us to critically examine our technique. I have made use of his work to suggest that the analyst's behaviour as seen by the patient can lead to a formulation of what I have called analyst-centred interpretations (Steiner 1994). However, what is missing from this late work is the subtle interactions between factors in the patient and those in the analyst and it is this which I find so interesting and so beautifully described by Rosenfeld in his prime.

My aim in this chapter is to try to show the excellence of Rosenfeld's work at its best, which I think exemplified a fine approach to psychoanalysis and to the analysis of transference in particular. A central aspect of this approach is the creation of a setting of sufficient stability to enable disturbing experiences to be contained, and since in my view, the setting includes the attitude of the analyst, this attitude is reflected in the way the analyst looks after and cares for the details of the setting. Rosenfeld would often argue, in his early work, that it was important to avoid anything which interferes with the development and understanding of the transference and he reported with some pride that he was able to analyse even the most disturbed psychotic patients while maintaining an analytic approach.

If the setting is reasonably established the analyst is free to explore the transference as it evolves in both its positive and negative manifestations. Moreover it is often only after prolonged and seemingly futile analytic work that a deeper understanding reveals positive feelings hidden beneath a predominantly negative transference and negative feelings discernable in the positive transference. I particularly admire the subtle observations and balance which characterised Rosenfeld's work at its best, when he could so wonderfully put himself in the patient's position without losing his analytic perspective.

I believe this is missing in his late work which can nevertheless serve a useful purpose since it reminds us how important it is for the analyst to scrutinise his work and to ask himself questions about his technique. If *Impasse and Interpretation* is seen not simply as a guide to good analytic work, but as an exposition of problems found in the analyst, then the points he makes can be learned from.

I will end by an illustration of just how complex the interaction of analyst and patient contributions to impasse can be, and how sensitive to these interactions Rosenfeld could be even in his late work. In Chapter 7 of Impasse and Interpretation Rosenfeld describes a patient he calls Pauline (Rosenfeld 1980, 137–138), who broke off analysis in an impasse after she developed a concrete delusional system in which she believed that Rosenfeld was infatuated with her. She accused him of being critical of her longing to have a child and claimed that when she became pregnant he tried to induce her to have an abortion. She said it was obvious that he was sexually interested in her and made constant attempts to seduce her. An erotic transference was here transformed into an erotomania as it became projected and denied. Rosenfeld described how he carefully examined his attitude to her and could find no sign of physical attraction, but he acknowledged that he had initially believed that she was a talented person who should one day train and become a psychoanalyst herself. I think it was clear that he had become infatuated with the patient's mind rather than with her body and that she had correctly perceived his attitude of personal interest in her and had experienced this concretely as a sexual interest. Looking at the details of the case we can see the subtle way the patient was able to convince Rosenfeld of her talent in psychoanalysis and to conceal the psychotic nature of her thinking.

It is this type of subtle examination of transference, countertransference and the interaction between them which characterises Rosenfeld's work at its best and which the reader can find so richly illustrated in his classic work. In it he illustrated how even the most difficult patients can be worked with while retaining a respect for the analytic setting, in particular while maintaining an analytic attitude in which the analyst's mind is open to consider a variety of factors in both the patient and in the analyst.

References

Abraham, K. (1919) 'A Particular Form of Neurotic Resistance Against the Psychoanalytic Method', in trans. D. Bryan and A. Strachey, *Selected Papers of Karl Abraham* (1927), London: Hogarth Press, 303–11.

Abraham, K. (1924) 'A Short Study of the Development of the Libido, Viewed in the Light of the Mental Disorders', in trans. D. Bryan and A. Strachey, *Selected Papers of Karl Abraham* (1973), London: Hogarth Press, 418–501.

Bion, W. R. (1956) 'Development of Schizophrenic Thought', in *International Journal of Psychoanalysis*, vol. 37, 344–6; reprinted in *Second Thoughts* (1967), London: Heinemann, 36–42.

Bion, W. R. (1957) 'Differentiation of the Psychotic from the Non-psychotic Personalities', in *International Journal of Psychoanalysis*, vol. 38, 266–75; reprinted in *Second Thoughts* (1967), London: Heinemann, 43–6.

Bion, W. R. (1959) 'Attacks on Linking', in *Second Thoughts* (1967), London: Heinemann, 93–109.

Bion, W. R. (1962) *Learning from Experience*, London: Heinemann.

Feldman, M. (2000) 'Some Views on the Manifestation of the Death Instinct in Clinical Work', *International Journal of Psychoanalysis*, vol. 81, 53–65.

Freud, S. (1911) 'Psycho-analytic Notes on an Autobiographic Account of a Case of Paranoia (Dementia Paranoides)', in *SE*, vol. 12, 3–82.

Freud, S. (1941) 'Findings, Ideas, Problems', in *SE*, vol. 23, 299–300.

Grosskurth, P. (1989) 'An Interview with Herbert Rosenfeld', in *Free Associations*, vol. 10, 23–31.

Horney, K. (1936) 'The Problem of the Negative Therapeutic Reaction', in *Psychoanalytic Quarterly*, vol. 5, 29–44.

Kernberg, O. F. (1975) *Borderline Conditions and Pathological Narcissism*, New York: Jason Aronson.

Klein, M. (1946) 'Notes on Some Schizoid Mechanisms', in *International Journal of Psychoanalysis*, vol. 27, 99–110; reprinted in *The Writings of Melanie Klein* (1975), London: Hogarth Press, vol. 3, 1–24.

Klein, M. (1952) 'The Origins of Transference', in *International Journal of Psychoanalysis*, vol. 33, 433–8; reprinted in *The Writings of Melanie Klein* (1975), London: Hogarth Press, vol. 3, 48–56.

Klein, M. (1955) 'On Identification', in *New Directions in Psychoanalysis*, London: Hogarth Press, 309–45; reprinted in *The Writings of Melanie Klein* (1975), London: Hogarth Press, 141–75.

Klein, M. (1957) *Envy and Gratitude*, London: Tavistock, reprinted in *The Writings of Melanie Klein* (1975), London: Hogarth Press, vol. 3, 176–235.

Rey, J. H. (1988) 'That Which Patients Bring to Analysis', in *International Journal of Psychoanalysis*, vol. 69, 457–70.

Riviere, J. (1936) 'A Contribution to the Analysis of the Negative Therapeutic Reaction', in *International Journal of Psychoanalysis*, vol. 17, 304–20; reprinted in A. Hughes (ed.), *The Inner World and Joan Riviere: Collected Papers 1920–1958* (1991), London: Karnac, 134–53.

Rosenfeld, H. A. (1947) 'Analysis of a Schizophrenic State with Depersonalization', in *International Journal of Psychoanalysis*, vol. 28, 130–9; reprinted in *Psychotic States* (1965), London: Hogarth Press, 34–51.

Rosenfeld, H. A. (1949) 'Remarks on the Relation of Male Homosexuality to Paranoid, Paranoid Anxiety and Narcissism', in *International Journal of Psychoanalysis*, vol. 30, 36–47; reprinted in *Psychotic States* (1965), London: Hogarth Press, 34–51.

Rosenfeld, H. A. (1950) 'Notes on the Psychopathology of Confusional States in Chronic Schizophrenia', in *International Journal of Psychoanalysis*, vol. 31, 132–7; reprinted in *Psychotic States* (1965), London: Hogarth Press, 52–62.

Rosenfeld, H. A. (1952a) Notes on the Psychoanalysis of the Superego Conflict in an Acute Schizophrenic Patient', in *International Journal of Psychoanalysis*, vol. 33, 111–31; reprinted in *Psychotic States* (1965), London: Hogarth Press, 63–103; and also in M. Klein, P. Heimann and R. Money-Kyrle (eds), *New Directions in Psychoanalysis* (1955), London: Tavistock, 180–219.

Rosenfeld, H. A. (1952b) 'Transference Phenomena and Transference Analysis in an Acute Catatonic Schizophrenic Patient', in *International Journal of Psychoanalysis*, vol. 33; reprinted in *Psychotic States* (1965), London: Hogarth Press.

Rosenfeld, H. A. (1954) 'Considerations Regarding the Psychoanalytic Approach to Acute and Chronic Schizophrenia', in *International Journal of Psychoanalysis*, vol. 35, 135–40; reprinted in *Psychotic States* (1965), London: Hogarth Press, 117–27.

Rosenfeld, H. A. (1963) 'Notes on the Psychopathology and Psycho-Analytic Treatment of Schizophrenia', in *American Psychiatric Association Psychiatric Research Report* No. 17; reprinted in *Psychotic States* (1965), London: Hogarth Press, 155–68.

Rosenfeld, H. A. (1964a) 'The Psychopathology of Hypochondriasis', in *Psychotic States* (1965), London: Hogarth Press, 180–99.

Rosenfeld, H. A. (1964b) 'The Psychopathology of Drug Addiction and Alcoholism', in *Psychotic States* (1965), London: Hogarth Press, 128–43.

Rosenfeld, H. A. (1964c) 'On the Psychopathology of Narcissism: A Clinical Approach', in *International Journal of Psychoanalysis*, vol. 45, 332–7; reprinted in *Psychotic States* (1965), London: Hogarth Press, 169–79.

Rosenfeld, H. A. (1969) 'On the Treatment of Psychotic States by Psychoanalysis: An Historical Approach', in *International Journal of Psychoanalysis*, vol. 50, 615–31.

Rosenfeld, H. A. (1971a) 'A Clinical Approach to the Psychoanalytic Theory of the Life and Death Instincts: An Investigation into the Aggressive Aspects of Narcissism', in *International Journal of Psychoanalysis*, vol. 52, 169–78.

Rosenfeld, H. A. (1971b) Contribution to the psychopathology of Psychotic Patients. The importance of projective identification in the ego structure and object relations of the psychotic patient. In P. Doucet and C. Laurin (eds), *Problems of Psychosis*, Amsterdam: Excerpta Medica; reprinted in Spillius Bott E. (1988) *Melanie Klein Today. 1. Mainly Theory*, London: Routledge, 117–37.

Rosenfeld, H. (1972) 'A Critical Appreciation of James Strachey's Paper on the Nature of the Therapeutic Action of Psychoanalysis', in *International Journal of Psychoanalysis*, vol. 53, 455–61.

Rosenfeld, H. A. (1975) 'Negative Therapeutic Reaction', in P. L. Giovacchini (ed.), *Tactics and Techniques in Psychoanalytic Therapy*, New York: Jason Aronson, vol. II, 217–28.

Rosenfeld, H. A. (1978a) 'Some Therapeutic Factors in Psychoanalysis', in *International Journal of Psychoanalytic Psychotherapy*, 7, 152–64.

Rosenfeld, H. (1978b) 'Notes on the Psychopathology and Psychoanalytic Treatment of Some Borderline Patients', in *International Journal of Psychoanalysis*, vol. 59, 215–21.

Rosenfeld, H. A. (1979) 'Difficulties in the Psychoanalytic Treatment of Borderline Patients', in J. Le Boit and A. Capponi (eds), *Advances in the Psychotherapy of the Borderline Patient*, New York: Jason Aronson.

Rosenfeld, H. A. (1981) 'On the Psychopathology and Treatment of Psychotic Patients (Historical and Comparative Reflections)', in J. S. Grotstein (ed.), *'Do I Dare Disturb the Universe?' A Memorial to W. R. Bion*, Beverly Hills: Caesura Press, 167–80.

Rosenfeld, H. A. (1983) 'Primitive Object Relations', in *International Journal of Psychoanalysis*, vol. 64, 261–7.

Rosenfeld, H. A. (1987) *Impasse and Interpretation*, London: Tavistock.

Segal, H. (1950) 'Some Aspects of the Analysis of a Schizophrenic', in *International Journal of Psychoanalysis*, vol. 30, 268–78; reprinted in *The Work of Hanna Segal* (1981), New York: Jason Aronson, 101–20.

Segal, H. (1956) 'Depression in the Schizophrenic', in *International Journal of Psychoanalysis*, vol. 37, 339–43; reprinted in *The Work of Hanna Segal* (1981), New York: Jason Aronson, 121–30.

Segal, H. and Steiner, R. (1987) 'H. A. Rosenfeld (1910–1986)', in *International Journal of Psychoanalysis*, vol. 68, 415–19.

Spillius, E. Bott (1988) *Melanie Klein Today. 1. Mainly Theory*, London: Routledge.

Steiner, J. (1993) *Psychic Retreats: Pathological Organisations of the Personality in Psychotic, Neurotic, and Borderline Patients*, London: Routledge.

Steiner, J. (1994) 'Patient-Centered and Analyst-Centered Interpretations: Some Implications of Containment and Countertransference', in *Psychoanalytical Inquiry*, vol. 14, 406–22.

Steiner, J. (2003) 'Gaze, Dominance, and Humiliation in the Schreber Case', in *International Journal of Psychoanalysis*, vol. 85, 269–84.

Steiner, J. (2006) 'Seeing and Being Seen: Narcissistic Pride and Narcissistic Humiliation', in *International Journal of Psychoanalysis*, vol. 87, 939–51.

Part II

Four papers by Herbert Rosenfeld

Chapter 7

Analysis of a schizophrenic state with depersonalization[1][¶]

Herbert A. Rosenfeld

INTRODUCTION

The patient I shall now discuss was sent to me for a variety of physical complaints of a functional origin. In the course of treatment it became apparent that I was dealing with a psychosis of the schizophrenic type. In this paper I shall concentrate only on certain aspects of the case; namely, the schizoid symptomatology and some of the schizoid mechanisms encountered. An additional aim will be to throw some light on depersonalization, and I will try to show the connection between processes of ego-disintegration and depersonalization.

SHORT HISTORY OF THE CASE

My patient, Mildred, is a young woman who was twenty-nine when the treatment started in March 1944. She is of average height and build, with straight fair hair. Her face is not exactly plain, but it usually appeared so because of its lack of expression. During the latter part of the treatment her expression became more alive and she sometimes smiled. She had her first breakdown in health when she was seventeen. Her second breakdown occurred at the age of twenty-five, in the early part of the war, while she was serving in the Auxilliary Territorial Service. She developed one physical illness after another, e.g. influenza and sore throats, until she had to be invalided from the Service. After some time she recovered and made another attempt to defeat the recurring illnesses by joining the Land Army, but again the physical disturbances prevented her from continuing. When I saw her in March 1944 for consultation she had been suffering from a so-called influenza for about four or five months. She agreed to analysis; we soon

1 Based on a paper read at a meeting of the British Psycho-Analytical Society, March 5, 1947.
¶ First published as 'Analysis of a Schizophrenic State with Depersonalization', in *International Journal of Psychoanalysis*, vol. 28, 130–9; reprinted with permission.

realized, however, that she had no desire to come for treatment, and this was in the main due to a deep-seated hopelessness about any recovery.

FAMILY AND EARLY HISTORY

There were no known schizoid disorders in the family, but one uncle is an alcoholic, and her father has suffered from a neurosis all his life. The patient described him as avoiding company and depending a great deal on his wife. She thought him old-fashioned, extremely dominating and very 'nervy'. She had always disliked him, but had, for the most part, ignored him. During the treatment her relationship with him improved considerably. She had always been very much attached to her mother, and had turned to her frequently in her childhood troubles. As a child she wrote poems and fairy stories and always found her mother a ready audience, and an adult who would treat her as an equal. She had one brother, Jack, nineteen months younger, and a sister, Ruth, six years younger.

Jack seems to have been a very attractive and intelligent boy, adored by everybody. Mildred, however, was ambivalent, but on the whole very fond of him and depended on him a great deal. She had quite consciously tried to adopt his personality and his interests, but had failed. When Jack was killed in a flying accident round about Christmas, 1940, she did not feel anything about it at the time; but during treatment she began to realize what a shock his death had been to her, and how responsible she felt for it. Her sister was very neurotic, suffering as a child from many anxieties, and as long as Ruth was small, Mildred felt quite motherly towards her, which enabled her to accept, without much jealousy the greater attention which was shown to the anxious little sister. In contrast to Mildred, Ruth improved when she got older, and during the war did very well in the Women's Auxiliary Air Force. Socially, too, she became more self-confident; but both these circumstances roused considerable jealousy in my patient.

About Mildred's early development nothing abnormal was reported to me. I gathered that she cried but little as an infant and apparently showed no reaction on being weaned. We must remember, however, that schizoid reactions in small children are generally overlooked and we often get a history of a particularly good baby, as in this case. She started to talk and walk normally. In addition to her mother, who breast-fed her, she had a nurse who was very devoted to her. As she was born in 1915, she did not see much of her father, who served all through the 1914–18 war; but whenever he was on leave he took a great deal of interest in his little daughter. When she was nineteen months old, Jack was born, and for three weeks her mother was away in a nursing home. This was the first time Mildred was separated from her mother for any length of time, and it was not until the tenth day that Mildred was allowed to visit her and the baby. Her mother told her later on that from the time she first saw Jack she became completely silent and withdrawn; and this reaction had disturbed the mother very much, since up to that time the child had talked normally. Four weeks after Jack's birth Mildred's nurse left to get married, and the new nurse had mainly to look after Jack. During the following years there were frequent changes of nurses. Mildred disliked them all, complaining to me that they treated her cruelly and often hit her, which might have been true, because she must have been an extremely difficult child to handle. She was frequently told she was no good, while Jack was held up to her as an example of goodness.

I had the impression that there was not only an impairment in her development after Jack's birth, but a definite regression to an earlier level of development. Not only did she give up speaking for a considerable time, but her ability to walk suffered as well, so that Jack developed far in advance of her. When Mildred was six a governess arrived, who seems to have been very prim and proper, but was liked by both children for her other good qualities. At eight years of age, Mildred fell ill with mastoiditis and had to have two operations, which greatly increased her paranoid reactions. She remembers feeling that for no apparent reason the doctors descended on her to frighten and hurt her, and afterwards she never quite overcame her fear of doctors. It took her many months to recover from these operations, and when she was better again she had to face another hard blow. Jack had been sent to school and they were no longer educated together.

She was educated at home by the governess, and for a long time she found it impossible to learn. Only when she was about twelve years of age did her intellectual capacity develop once more, and then she went to boarding-school, where she got on well, sometimes reaching the top of the class. On leaving school, she had a breakdown, which consisted in one physical illness after another, and culminated in a period of uncontrollable crying. The analysis revealed that jealousy of her best school friend, who got on better than she did, started this breakdown more than a year before leaving school. After school, until shortly before the war, she lived at home and was allowed to do exactly what she wanted. On the whole she felt fairly well, read a great deal; but took no interest in the running of the house. She had frequent periods of withdrawal from both friends and parents, and at these times she felt physically unwell, spending most of the time in bed. In addition, her mental state was always worse at the time of her periods when she suffered great discomfort and pain. As was mentioned earlier, she afterwards served in the A.T.S. and in the Women's Land Army.

CONDITION WHEN FIRST SEEN AND DURING EARLY STAGE OF TREATMENT

When I saw her first, she was living in a large flat in London with her parents, and for some considerable time she continued to be withdrawn from the family life, leaving all the work of the flat to her mother and an elderly maid. Though consciously very fond of her mother, during analysis we realized that she tried to keep her mother completely under her control, ignoring her wishes to be assisted, even when the latter was not feeling well. On the other hand, she wanted her mother to look after her, and give her her meals in bed, if she herself felt unwell. She expected her mother to take an interest in whatever she was doing, but she could stand no criticism from her nor even a suggestion or question referring to anything she might be doing. For example, she did not allow her mother to ask her whether she intended to stay in bed for the day or not, and when she was engaged in some occupation, such as reading, even a comment would be resented. If her mother did make one, Mildred immediately lost any desire to continue what she was doing, and would withdraw into herself. I later found out that there was a gradual improvement in this attitude after about a year's analysis.

Shortly after starting treatment she took up work again, doing some hours at an aircraft factory, and later on she succeeded in getting afternoon work at a well-known bookshop. Her physical health improved gradually and she attended analysis quite regularly, even while she had her periods, though at times she was very late. There were great difficulties with free association, and these increased rather than decreased. She generally made a long pause at the beginning of the hour, and at times she was silent for the whole session or only said a few words at the end. Sometimes the lack of material made it necessary to interpret on only one sentence. In addition, previous interviews or observations on her general behaviour had to be used for interpretations which were frequently of only a tentative character, and this created difficulties in assessing her reactions in the working through period. Only on very rare occasions did she succeed in talking fairly fluently for most of the session, and then she spoke predominantly of actual events in the past or present.

Another technical difficulty was a particularly strong resistance to interpretations connecting together material of several interviews, because she could very seldom consciously remember what had been discussed at previous sessions.[2] This made it difficult to obtain the conscious and intellectual co-operation which is so helpful in those schizoid disorders when the intellect is little affected.

THE DEPERSONALIZATION

Her conscious behaviour in analysis was marked by a rigid detachment and denial of all feelings, an attitude which at rare intervals was interrupted by

---

2 This attitude reminds one of Eidelberg's (1935) depersonalized patient who could not remember any previous interpretations and at times gave the impression of being demented.

paranoid suspicions or by despair about her lack of progress. Already at an early stage of the analysis she described symptoms and sensations of a distinctly schizoid type and feelings of depersonalization. She felt dim and sleepy, half unconscious and could hardly keep awake. At times when describing her experience she would say that there was something like a blanket separating her from the world, that she felt dead, or not here, or cut off from herself. At other times she called these feelings 'deadlock feelings', and explained that they had increased a few months before the treatment had started. She had felt giddy and faint at the time too.[3] She was frequently afraid of not being able to speak at all and of getting into a completely unconscious state. I realized that she was aware of the danger of insanity, because she said if she tried to join up with herself she might force her mind completely out of joint.

I have the impression that although this state occurred frequently as a defence against impulses of all levels it was also, indeed perhaps mainly, a defence against feelings of guilt, depression and persecution. From time to time there seemed a small improvement in her condition, but the slightest difficulty, particularly any positive transference interpretation, produced long-lasting silences, and when she was able to speak again she related that she had experienced some of the schizoid symptoms I enumerated just now. As usual there was an amnesia of everything we had discussed previously. Her inability to deal particularly with positive transference interpretations had its basis in her marked ambivalence, which I shall discuss more fully later on.[4] Whenever the opportunity arose I interpreted her love and hate impulses towards the analyst, but I had to dose these interpretations very carefully because of the seriousness of the schizoid reactions which followed. The positive transference towards the analyst as a parent, sister or brother figure was always displaced on to other people; but her object-relations at this stage were very insecure, and on analysis it turned out that more often than not the other people represented a part of herself.

To give a short example of this process: Denis, the husband of her best friend, had a nervous breakdown while he was separated from his wife who was expecting her second child. He tried his best to seduce my patient. At first she had great difficulty in controlling him. The wish to take him away from his wife soon came up as a conscious impulse, but it did not seem that

---

3 It is interesting to note that both Dr Mayer-Gross (1935) and Dr Shorvon (1946) in their papers on depersonalization point out that the beginning of the depersonalization syndrome is often marked by feelings of faintness and giddiness.

4 It is of interest to note that one of Reik's (1927) patients became depersonalized whenever Reik tried to make conscious her positive feelings to her husband, to whom her relationship was consciously a bad one.

she had any difficulty in coping with this wish directly. Her whole anxiety turned on whether she could control his wishes and arguments. She repeated some of his arguments to me, and it was clear that Denis stood for her own greedy sexual wishes which she had difficulty in dealing with and which she therefore projected on to him. Denis seemed a particularly suitable person for projection, because the precipitating factor of his neurosis corresponded to my patient's early situation, when the birth of her brother precipitated her first breakdown. The analysis of this mechanism helped Mildred to cope with Denis without having to avoid meeting him. Apart from the projection of impulses which were felt by the patient to be bad, there was a continuous projection of good impulses also into other people, particularly women friends, who not only represented good mother-figures, but the good part of herself. She felt excessively dependent on these friends and could hardly function without them. Her great dependency on Jack, which led to her inability to learn without him, was probably of the same nature.

DETAILS OF THE ANALYSIS

Coming now to the details of the actual analysis, I shall bring forward the instances mainly in chronological order, but it will be understood that I have to select points from a vast collection of material, and I am trying to choose only that which is most relevant to the main theme of my paper. In the winter of 1944–5 the patient developed influenza for the first time since she started treatment. She was afraid that the illness would drag on for months, but it cleared up in the normal time. When she returned to analysis, she told me she had found out quite a lot about the meaning of the influenza, namely, that she liked her 'flu' and enjoyed staying in bed and withdrawing from the world. She spontaneously described phantasies of living warmly and comfortably inside another person which she thought must be her mother, and remembered that she always told her mother that she had not wanted to be born. She herself related her overwhelming desire to go to sleep, or to become unconscious, to this particular state, and she admitted that she sometimes simply could not bear to remain awake and had to disappear into unconsciousness.[5]

This part of the analysis had a distinctly good effect on her physical symptoms; her difficulties then concentrated mostly on getting up in the morning to come to analysis at 10.30 a.m. For weeks she appeared up to forty minutes late. At first she seemed quite unworried about her inability

---

5 Other analysts, for example Nunberg (1924) and Reik (1927), have described phantasies of living inside the mother's womb in depersonalized patients.

to co-operate. Only gradually was I able to show her the anxiety which was hidden underneath her lack of feeling, and she then started to complain in these words: 'There is nothing to make me get up and come for treatment.' I was at first not sure what she meant by this oft-repeated complaint. Then one day she came almost in tears. She had asked her mother to give her breakfast in bed; she hoped that with her breakfast inside her she would be able to get up. But when she got it, it did not work, and she said: 'It is no good to make it up in all sorts of ways'. I analysed this incident and similar ones in terms of internal and external object-relationships, and felt that her difficulties were mainly due to a failure in introjecting and maintaining a good inner object as represented by the breakfast. Her complaint that there was nothing to make her get up would therefore mean there was no good inner object inside her to help her to get up; the breakfast was supposed to fill this gap but had failed.

Shortly after this she told me another spontaneous phantasy, which she had had since childhood and which she related now to her difficulties in co-operating. She felt there was a devil who attacked what she called the good people and was keeping them tied up in dungeons. They could not move and had gags in their mouths. No sooner did they manage to get a little freer than the devil appeared, attacked the victims violently and tied them up even more tightly than before. The victims were not killed, yet it was uncertain whether they were still alive. There was no point in fighting this devil because he was stronger than everybody. The only possible method of defence against him was to ignore him. This phantasy threw a light on the very strong negative therapeutic reaction of the patient which followed any improvement or freeing of her personality; it foreshadowed the depth of the paranoid situation which was to be expected in the analytic transference, when the analyst would turn into the devil father. For a while there was an improvement in her ability to come in time for treatment, and the positive transference then appeared, displaced, as always, on to a young relative whom she scarcely knew. After she heard that he was engaged, she felt very disappointed and became afraid of not being able to control her tears during the analytic session. She explained that if she started to cry she might not be able to stop again and would feel very ill. For a week she would not disclose the reason for her sadness. The hour after admitting what had happened, she felt dead and had lost her feelings so completely that she could not believe that she had ever had any love feelings before. When I interpreted to her the strength of her love and hate, her fear of not being able to control them, and that she was defending herself against depression, she was at first incredulous and felt I was only reassuring her that she had feelings. By the end of the hour she realized that she was warding off feelings of pain and said: 'It is like squeezing one's finger in a door and saying one didn't feel anything'. In this situation the deperson-alization was very marked. It followed a disappointment and appeared to be a mechanism of defence against depression. But this view appeared later on to be incomplete.[6]

During the next interview the depersonalization increased and was accompanied by feelings of persecution and sensations of being split in two. She talked about her fear of doctors and later on my talking was felt as an attack, making her feel I was pushing her into a hole, putting a lid over her and leaving her there. As a result of this assault she felt dead and although there was another part of her which was alive, the live part and the dead part did not know anything of each other. The connection of this material with the devil phantasy where the objects were put into dungeons was obvious, and it seemed that the persecuting devil attacked not only her objects but her very self. After the attack her ego was completely divided. I did not interpret this to my patient in detail at the time, as she was quite incapable of following any elaborate interpretation of mechanisms until the later part of treatment, I confined myself here to demonstrating to her her ambivalent impulses, which made her feel split in two. In the following weeks, I expected the depression relating to the disappointment she had experienced over the marriage of her friend to come more to the surface. But instead she began to slip from a state of depersonalization gradually into a schizophrenic state, which was marked by the development of a strongly paranoid relationship to the analyst.

At the beginning of this schizoid period she was not entirely devoid of positive feelings, but these she split off and transferred on to a girl friend, with whom she went out frequently and who arranged parties for her. She told me nothing about this at the time. To make the division complete, nothing good was allowed to mix with anything bad and, as I was kept and thought of as almost entirely bad, she acted accordingly. She began to stay away from treatment, sometimes for two or three days on end, and when she did come she was often thirty to forty-five minutes late. At times she appeared confused and disconnected, and her forgetfulness concerning matters in the analysis was most marked. Occasionally she could admit her feelings of persecution and explained that she didn't tell me anything which mattered to her because either I would make it bad or take it away from her, or would cause her feelings about it to disappear. She was trying to sort things out in her mind. I was muddling it all up. Whenever and whatever I interpreted she firmly believed and felt that I was telling her to stop thinking about what she had in her mind and trying to make her think of something else. Her greatest suspicion was that I was making her think entirely in my way, so that she no longer knew what she had thought of before, and that thus she would lose her own self.

---

6 Particularly Reik (1927) and Feigenbaum (1937) have emphasized depersonalization as a mechanism of defence.

Acute fears appeared that when she met people she might one day find herself talking in a strange voice or accent. This voice would have talked, I am certain, with the analyst's voice and accent, but the patient could not admit this connection consciously. About this time she frequently criticized her father for his selfishness and greed in his relationship to her mother and she herself could hardly bear speaking to him. Other material, for example, fears of hairy animals which attacked her, suggested the fear of an aggressive penis. Generally speaking, her persecutory fears were related to a bad father or penis and the sadistic impulses were mostly of an oral and anal nature. But the central anxiety was a phantasy of the persecuting analyst forcing himself into her to control her and rob her, not only of her inner possessions, for instance, her babies and her feelings, but her very self. It was not clear whether in this particular anxiety situation, I always stood for the bad father, or another figure. At this point of the analysis the girl friend she depended on was called up for war service, and her difficulties in coming for treatment and in speaking grew still worse. I realized that frequently she was not sufficiently aware of herself to come or talk or peform any action at all. At times she was more integrated, consequently more aware of herself. She was then able to complain that she felt so split up, and at times could not connect up enough to think or even talk. To get up or go to bed took her sometimes two hours because of the difficulty of consecutive action. Her sense of time was very confused. She could not judge time and often left home only shortly before or even after she was due to be at my house.

At the height of this transference-psychosis there was an alternative state to this split-up condition. She gave one the impression of being withdrawn into an omnipotent world of her own, where she was quite oblivious of external reality, where time and the passing of time did not matter, where she felt comfortable and not at all anxious about her serious mental condition. But sometimes she gave herself away and showed she was in fact controlling a severe threat coming from external reality. So she stated that she had a great deal to think about by herself, but she could not bring herself to tell it to me, because it would give me a handle with which to approach her and make her talk. This omnipotent withdrawal seemed very similar to the one she described in connection with influenza, when she admitted phantasies of living inside mother. But the force behind these phantasies seemed now increased. Indeed one sometimes had the feeling, when she showed no response, that she lived far away in another world.

I must admit that the alternation of states of narcissistic withdrawal and ego-disintegration seemed to me for some time a problem which I was unable to solve. In spite of the difficulties, I adhered all the time to the analytic technique in the hope that gradually a clearer pattern would show itself in the analytic situation. My understanding of the psychopathology of the schizoid mechanisms of my patient was very fragmentary at this point of the analysis, and her difficulties in co-operation did not make the task any easier. I was struck by the various phenomena I have been describing, but thought mainly of them as a defence against depression and persecution. Only gradually did I begin to realize the specific nature of the primitive schizoid processes which seemed to affect the very core of the ego. Fortunately the analysis somehow or other continued in spite of her short and rare appearances for the sessions. I am sure she must have unconsciously taken in some of my interpretations, but outwardly it appeared as if I were talking to a blank wall. Only quite gradually did she begin to show some response and understanding. She explained one day that she had realized that she could not stand coming for a treatment which made her aware of herself and the hopeless condition she felt herself to be in. Her fear of analysis failing was approached by her in a roundabout way. She expressed fears of losing her job at the bookshop where she had been working for just a year. She explained to me that in her life everything started to go wrong after one year and that after eight or nine months more she always had to give in. As at that time she had been under treatment for exactly nineteen months I could demonstrate to her convincingly that her greatest deeply denied fear at the present moment was that I would not continue with her analysis. You will remember that she was nineteen months old when her brother Jack was born and we realized in analysis that his birth meant to her that everything had come to an end and that her parents, particularly her mother, had given her up. The realization of the repetition of the early childhood situation struck her forcibly. This produced a flicker of hope and a slightly more positive attitude to the treatment. During the following weeks the pattern of the transference showed that after any particularly successful interview, when I was able to demonstrate to her some important connections, she stayed away or did not talk at the following session. I was struck by the similarity of her present reaction to what had actually happened at Jack's birth when she had become completely silent. I now understood that in the transference I was the mother, and any particularly productive hour represented for her my giving birth to a baby to which she reacted with complete silence and withdrawal. Consciously she still denied any hostility to the analyst, but in my interpretations I reminded her of the sadistic envious attacks of the devil who, in her phantasy, always attacked the good objects; and I tried to show her that she was now behaving like the sadistic devil and that attacks against me as the envied and admired mother were hidden behind her silence.

These interpretations were, as always, at first ignored, but in the very lengthy working-through period she admitted that she had always been afraid of letting her women friends down. She gave me an important example of this. In the Land Army her friend Mary and she had arranged to form a partnership in looking after the cows. She herself had undertaken the milking, but Mary was to be in charge of the scheme. She remembered that she had felt that in one way or another she would let Mary down. Actually they never worked together because she broke down, and now she could offer the explanation herself. She thought it was the fear of hurting Mary which made her ill. The analysis of this incident with Mary, which went on for months, revealed that she was mainly afraid that she would not get up in the morning to milk the cows. She had dreams of forgetting about the cows for days, which meant that all the good and nourishing milk was wasted, and pain was inflicted on the animals. I suggested that Mary stood for the mother and the cows for the breasts. In addition, this situation showed a distinct similarity to the transference situation, when she stayed away and refused to take in the nourishing analysis. From this I concluded that I not only represented the pregnant mother, and the mother who gave birth to Jack, but a part object, namely, the breast which she attacked in a particularly aggressive and tantalizing way by refusing to take any milk. I had the impression that these attacks on the breasts sprung not only from the jealousy of Jack, who was breast-fed by her mother, or from a deeply-repressed phantasy of having stolen Jack from the mother, but it seemed that early sadistic impulses against the breasts had been revived.[7] The incident with Mary was not, of course, the only example of her difficulties with women. She admitted now that she often withdrew from her girl friends in the same way as she reacted to me in analysis. Formerly she had depicted herself as being in harmonious and idealized relationship with them.

In sorting out information I had obtained up to that time, I concluded that even as an infant Mildred's sadistic impulses must have been very powerful. She must have been still struggling with them without any great success when the mother became pregnant again. A positive bond with her father had developed early, but the birth of Jack had caused an acute disappointment, and had acted, in addition to the loss of her first nurse, as a severe trauma to the already weak ego threatening the whole organization of it. In consequence, the situation of Jack's birth and the separation from

---

7 In analysing other schizoid patients, I have frequently observed a revival of similar sadistic attacks on the breast in the transference situation, which first showed themselves in the patient's inability to talk and to co-operate. The sadism, which gradually came to the surface, was of a particularly tantalizing quality: the patient appeared continuously to try to rouse interest and enthusiasm in the analyst, only to frustrate him and discourage him as soon as he showed any response by an interpretation. In spite of the history of an early weaning trauma in most of these cases, the patient had actually never refused the breast or other food as a baby. On the contrary, some of the patients were described as model babies. I want to suggest here an explanation of this fact. The sadistic attacks and the refusal of the breast exist in the phantasies only of these babies, while fear of starvation on the one hand, and persecuting anxieties on the other, compel the child to submit to taking food. In the analytic situation, a great number of these deeply-repressed phantasies are acted out before becoming conscious, and constitute our most valuable information about the impulses at work in earliest infancy.

the mother were denied. The mother was idealized and at the same time omnipotently controlled. Part of her sadism was projected on to her father, in the typical way, who was thus turned into a violent devil persecutor, but regression to the early relationship to the breast, which caused a mobilization of the schizoid processes, absorbed the rest of her aggression. This method of absorbing aggression I shall show in some detail later on.[8]

Progress was now noticeable in that she came regularly and mostly in time, but in spite of the intellectual understanding of the aggressive impulses inside her, she still could not experience them as conscious feelings. However, we observed that whenever she had occasion to feel envy or frustration, some of the symptoms of depersonalization or ego-disintegration which I have described before, appeared. It seemed that the destructive impulses, instead of being registered by her ego as aggression and being directed outwards against an external object, turned against her own libidinal impulses, causing a lack of desire and feeling, as well as against her ego, producing varying degrees of splitting and thus disturbances in the function of her ego. During the height of the paranoid schizoid state for periods lasting some days, her ego more or less ceased to function in relation to the analyst. She had, therefore, been unable to come to the sessions, and when she did come she was unable to feel, think or talk. The improvement in her condition showed itself in that now, even when she was in a bad phase, the destructive impulses left part of her ego intact, which meant that self-observation, talking and simple action were possible. In consequence, the schizoid processes of internal splitting and excessive projection of impulses and parts of her ego could be observed in greater detail. One had to be continuously on the look-out for those parts of herself which she projected into other people, mainly her friends, her sister or the analyst, and also for internal splits, which showed themselves in a monotonous form of speaking, complete inability to speak, drowsiness or other difficulties like disturbances of thinking and acting.

There was a great resistance to any attempt to integrate the projected and split-off parts, even after the intellectual recognition of such a process. A great deal of hate was hidden behind this resistance. This hostility only gradually came more to the surface and was part of the destructive forces inside her which divided practically anything and everything. By this I mean that this division was not only observed between good and bad impulses and objects, or between what occurred inside her and in outer reality, but it seemed as if all thought-processes, actions and impulses were split into

---

8 The regression of my patient reminds me of Melanie Klein's (1946) suggestion that a regression from a later level to the paranoid position occurs frequently in cases where strong paranoid fears had impeded the normal working-through of the paranoid position. Federn (1928), on the other hand, suggests that depersonalization is directly based on a shock in early childhood through which the ego becomes permanently weakened.

innumerable parts, isolated from one another and kept in a state of division. The patient spontaneously referred to this condition as 'I am split up again'. The persistent interpretation of all the splits and divisions, wherever they were noticed, seemed to bring great relief to the patient; it stimulated integration and increased her hope of ultimate recovery. The splitting of thoughts and actions, showed itself particularly in relation to the analytic situation, for example, her frequent lateness for analysis arose from her dividing up her coming to analysis into many isolated part-actions. Getting up, dressing, having breakfast, the bus ride to the analysis and the analytical session itself were all acts which did not seem to her to have anything to do with one another; if she were early in getting up, it did not necessarily mean to say she would come in time. She might quite easily take an hour for dressing without any anxiety about it getting late. Then she might hurry over breakfast, only to wait a long time before deciding to leave for her appointment. Sometimes she arrived quite in time, but would not start to talk, and it seemed that the action of arriving for analysis had finished and there was now a gap. The action of talking to me had become split off, and there was no desire to talk. As I pointed out before, owing to this division into part-actions, very little conscious anxiety was felt by her about her failure to come for treatment, and no adjustment in time or learning from experience could be achieved until she could think of all the part-actions together as a single whole. Similar difficulties showed themselves in her everyday life. She frequently took a great deal of trouble to fix an appointment with her hairdresser, who lived half-an-hour away from her, only to muddle up the appointment by leaving home at the time she was due there. She had not forgotten that the journey took thirty minutes, but this fact and the action of travelling had become completely dissociated from one another. Frequently her emotional appreciation suffered through the splitting process, even later on in the analysis when she had greatly improved. It happened that her fiancé had to go to Bombay where riots had broken out and shooting attacks on British soldiers were reported. For days she was quite unconcerned about him, because the fact of his being in Bombay remained disconnected from the dangerous situation which existed there. When this split righted itself through the analysis, she felt a great shock of anxiety and her normal concern for her fiancé could come to the surface.

I have now chosen some material, from a time when she herself had become aware of her impulses, in order to demonstrate the turning inward of the aggression.

Throughout the treatment she had had a great desire to ask questions, but only a few of her questions were actually asked, because she knew I would only interpret them and this she could not stand. Improvement was also shown in her increased ability to ask questions, which were in themselves an important source of information concerning her wishes and anxieties, and they also threw light on her reactions to frustration. As soon as I started to interpret a question, she complained of feelings of deadness or could not remember what she had asked. This repeated itself frequently, until one day she realized and admitted that she was demanding an immediate answer from me. She said she felt cross and tense. But what was the point of wanting to ask questions if one did not get an answer. After that she fell into a long silence. When I interpreted that she had got rid of her feelings, she replied that she was pleased not to feel any tension; but soon after she showed her understanding of the danger of this mechanism by saying: 'If one wanted to get rid of one's curiosity one would just die, because one has no desire to live. It is not that one wants to die; one just dies'. Instead of attacking and destroying the analyst, the destructive impulses had turned against her desire to live, her libido, which left her half-dead, as it were, and so in a state of depersonalization.[9] The intensity of the ambivalence on this and other similar occasions suggested that the impulses were of a pregenital nature and her curiosity seemed to be primarily an oral impulse, while the aggressive impulses were linked with anal phantasies and symptoms. For instance, her desire to find out through looking or reading led frequently to indigestion; and once when I had interpreted her crossness as an attack on the analyst with fæces, she failed to appear for the next session. She explained later that she had become so constipated that, instead of coming to analysis, she had gone home to give herself an enema. Similar facts were over and over again demonstrated to the patient and gradually genital impulses appeared for the first time more clearly in the transference. For example, when she left the bookshop for her analytic interview she began to suspect the girls of thinking she went out to enjoy herself. After my interpretation that she felt she was coming to enjoy the analysis she fell asleep, but had a dream which she related to me on waking. The dream was that she held the lid of a teapot in her hand and felt it was getting larger through her touch – the lid had here a distinctly phallic significance.

In other ways too she began to show her feelings more openly. A boy-friend wrote her a farewell letter on leaving her which upset her very much, and for the first time she could quite openly allow herself to cry during the analytic session. But she could not bear to hear me speak because, as she said, it hurt her, jarred on her, felt like an attack splitting her up into a thousand pieces, as if one were to take a hammer and hit a drop of quicksilver. I suggested that her hate of the boyfriend who deserted her was here turning against her feelings and herself. In an attempt to save herself,

---

9 The importance of the ambivalent conflict in depersonalization was particularly realized by Reik (1927), who points out that the lack of feeling is connected with death wishes directed against the ego. He quotes the words of one of his patients: 'Instead of knowing you want to kill somebody else, you wipe yourself out'. Melanie Klein (1946) has recently described the turning of the destructive impulses against the ego as a schizoid mechanism.

however, the destructive impulses were projected on to the analyst instead of herself, and so the feelings of persecution from without returned. As was almost to be expected after this interview, she stayed away for a few days to work through her hate by herself; but when she returned she told me that she had just made the discovery that she felt ashamed of never having been able to feel or to show affection. This realization was still completely split off from the analytical experience, and there was then a struggle for a week or so to make her aware of the split, so that she was able to become conscious of the positive transference. When she was at last able to express gratitude, it was for the fact that it was now possible for her to feel for the first time a whole and a live person.

It was shortly after this time that she came to know a young man with whom she fell deeply in love. At the same time the jealousy of other women could become fully conscious. This was realized particularly in connection with a girlfriend who had introduced this young man to her. The relationship between her and the young man developed satisfactorily on both sides, and after several weeks they got engaged. He had to go abroad for two months and they arranged to get married after his return to England. She reacted to his going away with an acute attack of depersonalization. This situation coincided with my summer vacation and there were no signs of a spontaneous recovery when I saw her after the holiday. She had again lost all desire to talk or to come for treatment, at the same time all her feelings for her fiancé had disappeared. She had been crying for days before they had to separate, because she had been afraid that something might happen to him on his plane journey as a repetition of what had happened to her brother Jack. But when he actually had to go she had not felt anything, and now she wondered whether she loved him at all, because she could only feel a thrill about the prospect of getting married, but he did not seem to exist. She was worried about this state and keen to co-operate.

Apart from the lack of feeling, another symptom reappeared which she had mentioned only once before at the height of the psychotic state. She felt that she was swelling up like a balloon twelve times her own size. At the same time she felt she was only a tiny self inside this balloon. My patient described this state as most unpleasant and the only clue she gave me was that expectancy had something to do with it. If she expected something from another person or from herself or someone wanted something from her, this symptom greatly increased. This description recalled to me the time of her acute paranoid fears concerning the analyst, when she had been afraid that whenever he spoke to her or expected her to speak he would force himself into her. Her active impulses of wanting to force herself into people to dominate, use and empty them, which corresponded to her passive paranoid fears, had been particularly strongly repressed, denied, and split off. I had the distinct impression that one of the reasons why the aggressive impulses had so forcibly turned against her libido, was a fusion of the libidinal impulses with her primitive, greedy, dominating self, against which she felt a violent hatred. Before it had always been difficult to make her aware of wishes, because any desire was unconsciously related to this greedy part of herself which had to be suppressed.

At this stage of the analysis it was sometimes possible for her to admit her wishes, and she now realized that she did not want her fiancé to go abroad. The frustration connected with his going had stirred up her greedy aggressive wishes. They had taken the form of phantasies in which she was forcing her way into him to compel him to do what she wanted and at the same time she felt she was emptying him of all that was good in him.[10] The result of this greedy aggressive attack was that she felt herself to be inside him. The sensation of the big balloon was connected with the fact that the object she had forced herself into was dead, emptied through her oral demands and full of air through her anal controlling attacks. She felt dead through the projective identification with the object. On the other hand, the loss of the feelings lost through this process seemed to correspond with that part of herself and her libido which through the projection had become split off from herself. This at once became related to the transference. I pointed out to her the anxiety about being separated from me during the holidays and her anxiety about the analysis coming to an end after her marriage. But when I interpreted that these fears had increased her desire and greed for treatment and that she had phantasies too of forcing herself into me to get from me all she wanted she went into a long silence and I then wondered whether she could cope with what I had pointed out. At last she could speak again and said that she had felt immediately that my interpretations were right, but, with that realization, she had become so tired that she had lost consciousness for a few minutes; nevertheless had managed to get out of the state again by herself. We understood that this reaction was a confirmation of my interpretation and that this state of unconsciousness and complete loss of herself was connected with a fear of going completely into me and losing herself there. It struck me then that her present fear of losing her feelings and the depersonalization were only quantitatively different from the complete loss of herself in the schizoid state of disintegration. If in her greedy desires she felt that she completely entered into another object, she either went to sleep or felt severely split up. If smaller parts underwent the same process she still retained the awareness of herself and was only aware of loss of feelings.

---

10 Similar reactions in depersonalized patients have been described by D. W. Winnicott (1945). Federn (1928) discusses depersonalization as a direct actual disturbance of the narcissistic libido and suggests that in depersonalization regression to ego-boundaries of earlier times takes place, which gives rise to disturbances in ego-feeling. Melanie Klein (1946) has shown the connection of schizoid ego-splitting with projective identification.

I found a similar situation applying to the splitting processes inside the ego, which I have already described. Here, too, it appears to depend on the quantity and strength of the destructive forces turning against the self, whether depersonalization or a varying degree of ego-disintegration takes place. In the last few months of analysis other interesting material appeared. She admitted, after a long-lasting resistance, that she had been completely frigid in her attempted sexual relations with her fiancé. The frigidity was distinctly related to her feelings of depersonalization. We found that she had masturbation phantasies of being raped, which were closely related to her fears of the penis and other objects being forced into her. Interpretations which established the connection between her primitive oral phantasies and her depersonalization with later genital phantasies, themselves following the earlier pattern, brought great relief to my patient; this decreased her fear of her genital impulses and allowed them to come more to the surface, making a gradual simultaneous improvement of her depersonalization, her frigidity and her object-relationships become evident. Another fact became notice-able at the end of treatment. With the greater integration of her ego, the process of introjection came more into the open. Previously introjection had been largely overshadowed by projection mechanisms; or, to put it in another way, the process of introjection had become inhibited through the paranoid anxiety of objects being forced into her. It was particularly the decrease of these specific paranoid fears, through the understanding of the primitive impulses and processes described, which enabled the introjection mechanisms to function again.[11] When she got married and went with her husband to live abroad, the analysis had to be interrupted. I saw her a few times after her honeymoon. She was happy and confident, and her sexual relationship to her husband was developing satisfactorily.

From many points of view the analysis is still very incomplete and there is a danger of relapse. On the other hand, the marriage has a reasonable chance of success and since the patient will return with her husband in two or three years, I did not put any pressure on her to continue analysis at that time.

SUMMARY

I will briefly summarize my conclusions from the analysis of this case.

Schizoid processes, including depersonalization, can be used by the ego as a defence-mechanism at comparatively late stages of development. They are,

---

11 Melanie Klein (1946) has made similar observations, she points out: 'As a result of the mind or body being felt to be controlled by other people in a hostile way, there may be a severe disturbance in introjecting good objects'.

however, processes which affect the very structure of the ego, causing varying degrees of splitting and projection of the ego. These processes are related to the working within the ego of destructive impulses, which are felt to be alien (split off) and therefore persecutors. Oral and anal sadistic impulses, directed against the inside of mother's body, also increase the persecutory anxiety. These factors suggest an origin of these schizoid mechanisms on a paranoid level, which weakens the subsequent development of the ego. The weakened ego of my patient felt the birth of the brother and the circumstances related to it as a shock, and a considerable regression took place through which the schizoid processes became reinforced.

Depersonalization is still considered by psychiatrists and psychoanalysts alike as a very obscure subject. It is often found in the beginning or end of a neurosis or psychosis; it accompanies some organic diseases of the brain, schizophrenic conditions, depressions, obsessional neurosis, hysterical conditions, and has been described as a separate disease entity.

I have tried to show in this paper that there is a definite relationship between the schizoid process and depersonalization. The schizoid splitting mechanisms described were manifested both in the schizoid ego-disintegration and in the depersonalization of my patient. I suggest, therefore, that there is a quantitative difference only between the two clinical states. Among analysts, Helene Deutsch (1942) has drawn attention to certain emotional states similar to depersonalization, and their relationship to schizophrenia, and lately Melanie Klein (1946) has suggested that in depersonalization regression to the paranoid schizoid position takes place.

References

Bergler, E. and Eidelberg, L. (1935) 'Der Mechanismus der Depersonalisation', in *Internationale Zeitschrift für Psychoanalyse*, vol. 21, 258.

Deutsch, H. (1942) 'Some Forms of Emotional Disturbances and their Relationship to Schizophrenia', in *Psychoanalytic Quarterly*, vol. 11, 301[à].

Eidelberg, L. (1935) See Bergler.

Federn, P. (1928) 'Narcissism in the Structure of the Ego', in *International Journal of Psychoanalysis*, vol. 9, 403[à].

Feigenbaum, D. (1937) 'Depersonalization as a Defence Mechanism', in *Psychoanalytic Quarterly*, vol. 6, 4[à].

Klein, M. (1946) 'Notes on Some Schizoid Mechanisms', in *International Journal of Psychoanalysis*, vol. 27, 99[à].

Mayer-Gross, W. (1935) 'On Depersonalization', in *British Journal of Medical Psychology*, vol. 15, 103.

Nunberg, H. (1924) 'Ueber Depersonalisation-szustaende im Lichte der Libido-Theorie', in *Internationale Zeitschrift für Psychoanalyse*, vol. 10, 17.

Reik, Th. (1927) 'Psychologie und Depersonalisation', in *Wie man Psychologe wird*, Vienna, 34.

Shorvon, H. I. (1946) 'The Depersonalization Syndrome', in *Proceedings of the Royal Society of Medicine*, vol. 39, no. 12.

Winnicott, D. W. (1945) 'Primitive Emotional Development', in *International Journal of Psychoanalysis* vol. 26, 137[à].

Chapter 8

On the psychopathology of narcissism: a clinical approach[1][¶]

Herbert A. Rosenfeld

Freud was pessimistic about the psycho-analytic approach to the narcissistic neuroses. He felt that people suffering from these diseases had no capacity for transference, or only insufficient remnants of one. He described the resistance of these patients as a stone wall which cannot be got over, and said that they turn from the physician not in hostility but in indifference. Many analysts have tried to develop methods of analysis which would deal with narcissistic patients – I am thinking of Waelder (1925), Clark (1933), and later Fromm-Reichmann (1943), (1947), Bion (1962), Rosenfeld, and others. The majority of analysts who have treated narcissistic patients have disagreed with Freud's view that there was no transference. As the transference is the main vehicle for any analytic investigation, it seems essential for the understanding of narcissism that the behaviour of the narcissist in the analytic transference situation should be minutely observed.

Franz Cohn (1940) suggested that the sharp distinction between transference neurosis and narcissistic neurosis should be disregarded. He felt that the transference in the narcissistic neurosis is of a primitive or rudimentary type – for example, there are often serious difficulties in distinguishing between subject and object – and he stresses the introjection and projection of destructive tendencies in oral and anal terms in relation to the analyst. Stone (1954) described transferences which are 'literally narcissistic', where the analyst is confused with the self or is like the self in all respects: the therapist and the patient alternately seem to be parts of each other. He stresses both the primitive destructiveness and the need to experience the analyst as an omnipotent, godlike figure, and suggests that, in the patient's fantasy about the analyst's omnipotence, guilt about primitive destructive aggression plays an important part.

1 Read at the 23rd International Psycho-Analytical Congress, Stockholm, July–August 1963.
¶ First published as 'On the Psychopathology of Narcissism: A Clinical Approach', in *International Journal of Psychoanalysis*, vol. 45, 332–7; reprinted with permission.

Many of the observations made by Cohn (1940) and Stone (1954) seem to come close to my own investigation. I notice that in their description of the narcissistic transferences the terms primary and secondary narcissism are not used. Instead we meet with such terms as omnipotence, confusion of the self and objects, introjection of objects, projection of aggression into objects, insatiable demands towards objects, and nullification. The use of these terms in describing narcissistic patients seems valuable, but it appears to me important and necessary to define more clearly the nature of the relation to objects in narcissism and the particular defence mechanisms related to them. This may be a contradiction in terms, because for many analysts primary narcissism implies an objectless state. But we should remember that Freud regarded the oceanic feeling, the longing for union with God or the Universe, as a primary narcissistic experience. Federn (1929) in discussing primary narcissism describes the baby's craving for the mother's breast, but suggests that the object is as yet not external to the ego feeling. Abraham (1924) discusses limitless narcissism as a relation to an object in which, while the object is incorporated, the individual pays no attention whatever to the interests of his object, but destroys it without the least hesitation. Balint (1960) went so far as to suggest that what Freud described as primary narcissism should be called primary object love. I myself believe that much confusion would be avoided if we were to recognize that the many clinically observable conditions which resemble Freud's description of primary narcissism are in fact primitive object relations.

In narcissistic object relations omnipotence plays a prominent part. The object, usually a part-object, the breast, may be omnipotently incorporated, which implies that it is treated as the infant's possession; or the mother or breast are used as containers into which are omnipotently projected the parts of the self which are felt to be undesirable as they cause pain or anxiety.

Identification is an important factor in narcissistic object relations. It may take place by introjection or by projection. When the object is omnipotently incorporated, the self becomes so identified with the incorporated object that all separate identity or any boundary between self and object is denied. In projective identification parts of the self omnipotently enter an object, for example the mother, to take over certain qualities which would be experienced as desirable, and therefore claim to be the object or part-object. Identification by introjection and by projection usually occur simultaneously.

In narcissistic object relations defences against any recognition of separateness between self and object play a predominant part. Awareness of separation would lead to feelings of dependence on an object and therefore to anxiety. Dependence on an object implies love for and recognition of the value of the object, which leads to aggression, anxiety, and pain because of the inevitable frustrations and their consequences. In addition dependence stimulates envy, when the goodness of the object is recognized. The omnipotent narcissistic object relations therefore obviate both the aggressive feelings caused by frustration and any awareness of envy. When the infant omnipotently possesses the mother's breast, the breast cannot frustrate him or arouse his envy. Envy is particularly unbearable to the infant and increases the difficulty in admitting dependence and frustration. It seems that the strength and persistence of omnipotent narcissistic object relations are closely related to the strength of the infant's envy. Envy has omnipotent qualities; it seems that it contributes to the omnipotence of the narcissistic object relations while the envy itself may be simultaneously split off and denied. In my clinical observations of narcissistic patients the projection of undesirable qualities into the object plays an important part. The analyst is often pictured in dreams and fantasies as a lavatory or lap. This relationship implies that any disturbing feeling or sensation can immediately be evacuated into the object without any concern for it, the object being generally devalued. In severe narcissistic disturbances we can invariably see the maintenance of a rigid defence against any awareness of psychic reality, since any anxiety which is aroused by conflicts between parts of the self or between self and reality is immediately evacuated. The anxiety which is thus defended against is mainly of a paranoid nature, since narcissistic object relations date from earliest infancy when anxiety is predominantly paranoid.

Clinically, narcissistic object relations often appear to the analyst and are also experienced by the patient as very ideal and desirable object relations. For example the relation to the lavatory/mother in the analysis is frequently felt as ideal, because the patient feels relieved when everything unpleasant can be immediately discharged into the analyst during a session. When the patient claims to possess the analysis, as the feeding breast, he gives himself credit for all the analyst's satisfactory interpretations, a situation which is experienced as perfect or ideal because it increases the patient's feeling during the analytic session that he is good and important. Sometimes narcissistic patients picture themselves in a mutually satisfactory ideal relationship with the analyst where the identity of patient and analyst is not differentiated, a situation reminiscent of Freud's description of the oceanic feeling. Another instance of narcissistic idealization is the patient who feels that he is loved by everyone, or demands to be loved by everyone, because he is so lovable. All these patients seem to have in common the feeling that they contain all the goodness which would otherwise be experienced in a relationship to an object. We usually encounter simultaneously a highly idealized self-image, which dominates the analytic situation, and anything interfering with this picture is rigorously defended against and omnipotently denied.

I shall now illustrate some of the problems related to severe narcissism by bringing case material from a patient who showed a marked narcissistic transference without being overtly psychotic. There is nothing in the patient's history which would seem to account for his persistent narcissistic attitude. He is the son of fairly wealthy parents, and he has two sisters. He had apparently always managed superficially to get on quite well with people, and was successful at school because of his high intelligence. When he started treatment he had just married and he had some difficulties with his wife. Apart from an occasional feeling of oneness with her he was very jealous and intensely preoccupied with her relations with other people, men and women. The analysis revealed the depth of the patient's narcissism, his lack of emotional contact with other people, and, as a result, the lack of pleasure in his life which made him envious of everybody. He particularly envied his wife who, he felt, was far more capable than he was of enjoying relations with people, including himself. When I first saw the patient he appeared slightly withdrawn from reality and from other people, and had a vaguely superior and patronizing attitude which he tried to disguise. He admitted that he occasionally felt frustrated in personal relations, with friends and his young wife, but generally he blamed them for any difficulty which arose. He was very interested in being analysed in spite of the fact that he did not feel that he really needed analysis. He pictured himself almost immediately as the perfect patient who made enormous progress, but in fact he could make very little proper use of the analysis. He constantly projected his problems into his wife or other people, including the analyst, and was quite unable to experience them as belonging to himself. He enjoyed interpreting his own dreams in detail and explaining his thoughts and feelings, but any conflict, anxiety, or depression which emerged was so quickly discharged that it could barely be experienced. He did not resent interpretations, but on the contrary took them up quickly and talked about them in his own way, feeling very self-satisfied with his knowledge since he did not feel that the analyst had made any contribution. His attitude made it extremely difficult to effect any change in his personality, so that one felt up against a stone wall in a way reminiscent of Freud's description. Behind this stone wall there seemed to be omnipotence hiding hostility and envy, completely denied by the patient and difficult to demonstrate in the analytic material. After I had shown him again and again his avoidance of any close contact with myself or with his own feelings, particularly hostility towards me, he came to a session saying that he now wanted to get closer to his problems. He then told me a dream in which he and others were travelling in a very fast train. He suddenly saw a kind of surrealistic machine land near the train and send out towards it a wide ray of very dangerous fire. Luckily the train escaped this attack by quickly moving away, but there was a feeling that the attack would be repeated. The patient felt that this machine was sent over from Russia by a man who had apparently lived in England before but felt bitter and revengeful because of some ill treatment which he believed he had received. There was a feeling in the dream that some widespread attacks were going to be made on various places in England, mainly hotels with such names as Royal, Royalty, Majestic, Palace, etc., and yet that the attacks were being directed against his parents. There also seemed to be a food shortage. Two girls were in the train with him. In another part of the dream there were a number of girls leaning against a stone wall and prostituting themselves because of the food shortage. He approached one of them and said 'Would you like a customer?' but she only laughed, and he felt disappointed, since his approach was made seriously. In his associations he thought that the Russian must be associated with himself, as he felt sympathy with him as though the Russian had a right to make these attacks. He thought he must have hated his parents to be important and therefore felt slighted by them. He thought that the Russian must have wanted to be the most important person himself and that the attacks were a result of his feeling humiliated and therefore resentful. The patient had very little emotional reaction to the dream.

The dream shows very clearly the omnipotent virulence of an extremely hostile omnipotent part of his personality which makes attacks both on the important superior parents and on a part of himself. The reason for the attack is obviously derived from his babyhood envy of the important grown-ups because the parents, in his associations, are accused of humiliating him and making him feel small. It is also clear in the dream that the Russian has a paranoid grudge, which is an admission of his own paranoid attitude which is consciously denied. The train which moves quickly to avoid any contact with the destructive rays is related to his train of thought and his own self containing the two breasts (girls). In fact he prides himself on being able to move extremely quickly and cleverly, and so in his thoughts being able to avoid any contact with his destructive self. The dream implies that making contact with the analyst as an important parental figure arouses dangerous, envious, paranoid impulses. It is interesting in the dream, that the envious paranoid Russian is placed in the distance, while the destructiveness emanating from him influences the patient's train of thought, his contacts and relations to his parents and women. The dream shows clearly how in narcissistic relationships envy is split off and kept away from self-awareness, and at the same time the patient's destructiveness keeps his object relations devalued and so enables him to by-pass his difficulties. An interesting feature in the dream is the food shortage which makes the girls into prostitutes. This implies that the importance of the breast is denied, and women are devalued into prostitutes, who, lacking food or breasts, cannot feed themselves and therefore have to come to the patient to get money for food: this would also indicate a projection of the dependence into the prostitutes.

As the patient had started the session by saying that he had made up his mind to get on with the analysis, in other words wanted to come closer to me, it is clear that the dream reveals not only his attitude to women but to the analyst also. He deals with his fear of being rejected by me by approaching me – in a superior way turning me into a prostitute. It is interesting that the prostitutes lean against a stone wall, which would confirm that the stone wall of the narcissistic transference has to be linked with narcissistic object relations, which are emerging in the analysis.

Following this dream the patient's aggressive superiority towards the analyst was more openly admitted in dreams and associations, but his desire to possess the analysis and feel that it was his own creation was only admitted openly after the following dream. The patient was shopping, and was offered a special kind of salt packed in self-made containers. It was much cheaper than ordinary salt, only ninepence for four pounds. He asked the storekeeper whether it was as good as ordinary salt. In spite of the storekeeper's assurance that it was perfectly all right, the patient himself did not believe it. On leaving the shop it took him about two hours to get home, and he felt guilty because he was afraid that his wife would be waiting anxiously for him. The patient remarked that he had had to buy salt the day before because they had run out of it. He felt sure that the salt must have something to do with the analysis, as four pounds reminded him of coming four times a week to his sessions. He stressed that the salt was so much cheaper because obviously the people had made it up themselves. I could show the patient in this dream that ostensibly he comes to me to have analysis, but he maintains that what he gets from me is his own self-made version of the analysis which he pretends to himself is as good as the ordinary analysis. He obviously tries in the dream to get reassurance from the shopkeeper-analyst that this is right and normal, but he admits that he does not really believe this himself. Staying out late implies a projection into his wife of his feelings of dependence and the anxiety about having to wait. The dream illustrates that the patient has not as yet admitted to himself his dependence on me; it is denied and projected, and this continuously leads to acting out. I would like to add here the general meaning of the self-made version of the analysis, which is clearly represented in this dream, because it plays a very important part in the analysis of many narcissistic patients. While ostensibly the narcissistic patient maintains that he has a superior and sometimes more creative breast in his possession, which gives him better analysis and food than the mother-analyst could ever produce, careful analysis reveals that this highly valued possession of the patient represents his own faeces which have always been highly idealized, a fact carefully concealed by the patient. The unmasking of the situation, while it may temporarily lead to the patient's feeling severely deflated, is essential if real relations to external and internal objects are ever to be established.

In a later dream the patient illustrates how he entirely reverses the relationship to the analyst by omnipotent projective identifications. In the dream the patient was a doctor holding a surgery. He had a cake, and four women were coming to see him. He suspected that these women were only pretending that they were ill in order to get attention. There was some trouble on the roof of the house and he was starting to repair it. A noise was heard of something falling down, or of hammering, and at the first sound the women quickly withdrew, afraid that something might fall on them. In his associations the patient described the women as fat and greedy. The dream shows in an undisguised way that the patient has put himself in the role of the analyst who not only possesses the cake – the breast – but also does the reparative work. His own greedy attitude of simply wanting to get food from the analysis without really admitting that he is ill, and withdrawing from me quickly whenever I make an interpretation which might touch him, is projected on to the four women who, as often before, represent the analysis or the analyst (cf. the four pounds of salt). We notice that in the dream the patient has become more appreciative of the analyst and the reparative work of the analysis, and feels critical of his own greedy demands on the analyst and of his constant withdrawals whenever he hears an interpretation which he feels is good. However, he evacuates entirely his unsatisfactory attitude into the analyst, who in the dream is changed into the patient's unsatisfactory self, while he takes over the role of the analyst whom he admires.

I shall now go on to discuss some of the more practical considerations in the analysis of narcissistic patients. A powerful resistance in their analysis is derived from their superior omnipotent attitude, which denies any need for dependence and the anxieties related to it. This behaviour is often extremely repetitive, and there are many alternative versions which are used by the narcissistic patient. The intelligent narcissist often uses his intellectual insight to agree verbally with the analyst and recapitulates in his own words what has been analysed in previous sessions. This behaviour not only blocks any contact and progress, but is an example of the narcissistic object relation I have been describing. The patient uses the analytic interpretations but deprives them quickly of life and meaning, so that only meaningless words are left. These words are then felt to be the patient's own possession, which he idealizes and which gives him a sense of superiority. An alternative method is shown by patients who never really accept the analyst's interpretations, but constantly develop theories, which they regard as superior versions of analysis.

In the first case the patient steals the interpretations representing the breast from the analyst/mother, turning them into faeces; he then idealizes them and feeds them back to the analyst. In the second case the patient's own theories are produced as if they were idealized faeces, which are presented as food superior to the breast, which the analyst/mother provides. The main source of this resistance and behaviour comes from the narcissistic patient's denial of envy, which is only forced into the open when he has to recognize the analyst's superiority as a feeding mother. The patient whose dreams I have discussed here gradually admitted that he had to keep vague and uncertain that it was I who actually gave him the analysis, because any real clarity about my role led to unbearable feelings of his being small, hungry, and humiliated, which he deeply resented even when I was available. Occasionally resentment broke through, and the patient felt that I had all the answers and gave him only some. Why should he listen to me or depend on me if what I gave him was not complete? This resentment was derived from envious feelings against the analyst/mother who, possessing the breast, only feeds the child, instead of handing over the breast to him completely. At first such a breakthrough was only fleeting, and the patient guarded against such feelings by quickly putting himself into a superior position to me by thinking of something at which he excelled. There was a powerful resistence also from his ideal self-image which he was slowly able to describe in the following way: 'I want to feel good and have a perfect relation to you. Why should I admit anything bad which would spoil the good picture I have of myself, which I feel you must admire too?'

The rigid preservation of the ideal self-image blocks any progress in the analysis of narcissistic patients, because it is felt to be endangered by any insight and contact with psychic reality. The ideal self-image of the narcissistic patient may be thought of as a highly pathological structure based on the patient's omnipotence and denial of reality.

Only very slowly was the patient able to admit that the keeping up of the ideal self-image meant an elimination of all my interpretations which might endanger the perfect image of himself. He began to notice that he constantly lost contact with everything which had been discussed during the sessions. This was painful to him, but the pain was again quickly eliminated, despite the fact that it meant expulsion of the good experience with the analyst, which had led to the painful insight. This attitude is very characteristic of the narcissistic patient, and not only pain but insight is expelled again and again. For example, when my patient's need to be dependent came more to the surface, he at first projected the dependence into his wife and acted it out with her by creating a situation where she was depressed and in need. He then explained to her the reasons why she was depressed, and became angry when she did not immediately understand his interpretations and behave properly. However, he gradually became aware that this expulsion of his dependence, and thus insight, constantly created more difficulties and frustrations in his life. We discovered that whenever the patient acknowledged any real understanding about himself and tried not to project his feelings, he became anxious and depressed. At that moment he became confused and he heard himself saying, 'This is dangerous', in response to which he again expelled the anxiety, depression, and insight. I then showed him that what was endangered in such a situation was not his sane or good self but his omnipotent mad self. This struck him very forcibly, and he said it felt to him like driving in his car and coming up against a red light. This of course was a danger signal to stop, but he felt that his danger signal made him feel that he wanted merely to accelerate to get through the red light without stopping, in other words to get through the danger of being confronted with sanity and reality and back into his idealized omnipotent position.

CLINICAL PROGNOSIS

The clinical result of the analysis of a narcissistic patient depends on the degree to which he is gradually able to acknowledge the relationship to the analyst, representing the mother in the feeding situation. This implies an overcoming of some of the problems I have been describing and therefore a recognition of separation and frustration and a working through of what Melanie Klein has called the depressive position. We have also to take into account that some narcissistic patients have often a less narcissistic, a more normal object-directed part of the personality, and improvement has to be measured in terms of the integration of the narcissistic parts of the personality with this. To bring about an improvement, the omnipotent narcissism of the patient and all the aspects related to it have to be laid bare in detail during the analytic process and to be integrated with the more normally concerned part of the patient. It is this part of the analysis which seems to be so unbearable. Splitting results again and again when either the normal or the omnipotent parts of the self are denied. Often the attempt at integration fails because mechanisms related to the omnipotent narcissistic self suddenly take over control of the normal self in an attempt to divert or expel the painful recognition. However, there are patients who gradually succeed in their struggles against narcissistic omnipotence, and this should encourage us as analysts to continue our research into the clinical and theoretical problems of narcissism.

References

Abraham, K. (1924) 'A Short Study of the Development of the Libido, Viewed in the Light of Mental Disorders', in *Selected Papers* (1927), London: Hogarth.

Balint, M. (1960) 'Primary Narcissism or Primary Love', in *Psychoanalytic Quarterly*, vol. 29.

Bion, W. (1962) *Learning from Experience*, London: Heinemann.

Clark, L. P. (1933) 'Treatment of Narcissistic Neuroses and Psychoses', in *Psychoanalytic Review*, vol. 20.

Cohn, F. (1940) 'Practical Approach to the Problem of Narcissistic Neuroses', in *Psychoanalytic Quarterly*, vol. 9.

Federn, P. (1929) 'The Ego as Subject and Object in Narcissism', in *Ego Psychology and the Psychoses* (1953), London: Imago.

Federn, P. (1943) 'The Psychoanalysis of the Psychoses', in *Ego Psychology and the Psychoses*, London: Imago.

Freud, S. (1916–1917) 'Introductory Lectures', in *SE*, vols 15–16.

Fromm-Reichmann, F. (1943) 'Psychoanalytical Therapy with Psychotics', in *Psychiatry*, vol. 6.

Fromm-Reichmann, F. (1947) 'Problems of Therapeutic Management in a Psychoanalytic Hospital', in *Psychoanalytic Quarterly*, vol. 16.

Stone, L. (1954) 'The Widening Scope of Indications for Psychoanalysis', in *Journal of the American Psychoanalytic Association*, vol. 2.

Waelder, R. (1925) 'The Psychoses: Their Mechanisms and Accessibility to Influence', in *International Journal of Psychoanalysis*, vol. 6.

A clinical approach to the psychoanalytic theory of the life and death instincts: an investigation into the aggressive aspects of narcissism[1][¶]

Herbert A. Rosenfeld

When Freud introduced his dualistic theory of the life and death instincts in 1920 a new era in the development of psychoanalysis began which gradually opened up a deeper understanding of aggressive phenomena in mental life. Many analysts objected to the theory of the death instinct and were tempted to discard it as purely speculative and theoretical; however, others soon recognized its fundamental clinical importance.

Freud emphasized that the death instinct was silently driving the individual towards death and that only through the activity of the life instinct was this death-like force projected outwards and appeared as destructive impulses directed against objects in the outside world. Generally the life and death instincts are mixed or fused in varying degrees, and Freud maintained that the instincts, meaning the life and death instincts, 'hardly ever appear in "a pure form"'. While states of severe defusion of the instincts do resemble Freud's description of the unfused death instinct – for example, a wish to die or to withdraw into a state of nothingness – on detailed clinical examination we find that the death instinct cannot be observed in its original form, since it always becomes manifest as a destructive process directed against objects and the self. These processes seem to operate in their most virulent form in severe narcissistic conditions.

I shall therefore attempt in this paper to clarify particularly the destructive aspects of narcissism and relate this to Freud's theory of the fusion and defusion of the life and death instincts.

In Freud's writings following his more speculative approach in 'Beyond the Pleasure Principle', it became clear that he used the theory of the life and death instincts to explain many clinical phenomena. For example, in 'The Economic Problem of Masochism' (1924) he said:

1 Invited contribution to the 27th International Psycho-Analytical Congress, Vienna, 1971.
¶ First published as 'A Clinical Approach to the Psychoanalytic Theory of the Life and Death Instincts: An Investigation into the Aggressive Aspects of Narcissism', in *International Journal of Psychoanalysis*, vol. 52, 169–78; reprinted with permission.

Moral masochism thus becomes a classical piece of evidence for the existence of 'instinctual fusion': its dangerousness lies in its origin in the death instinct and represents that part of the latter which escaped deflection on to the outer world in the form of an instinct of destruction.

In the 'New Introductory Lectures' (1933) he discussed the fusion of Eros and aggressiveness and attempted to encourage analysts to use this theory clinically. He said:

> This hypothesis opens a line of investigation which may some day be of great importance for our understanding of pathological processes. For fusions may be undone and such defusions of instincts may be expected to bring about the most serious consequences to adequate functioning. But this point of view is still too new. No one has so far attempted to make practical use of it.

Only four years later, in 'Analysis Terminable and Interminable' (1937), Freud returned to the clinical application of his theory of the death instinct for the understanding of deep-seated resistances against analytic treatment, saying:

> Here we are dealing with the ultimate things which psychological research can learn about: the behaviour of the two primal instincts, their distribution, mingling and defusion. No stronger impression arises from the resistances during the work of analysis than of there being a force which is defending itself by every possible means against recovery and which is absolutely resolved to hold on to illness and suffering.

He linked this with his previous theory of the negative therapeutic reaction, which he had related to an unconscious sense of guilt and the need for punishment, now adding:

> These phenomena are unmistakable impressions of the power in mental life which we call the instinct of aggression or of destruction according to its aims and which we trace back to the original death instinct of living matter . . . Only by the concurrent or mutually opposing action of the two primal instincts – Eros and death instinct – never by one or the other alone, can we explain the rich multiplicity of the phenomena of life.

Later on in the same paper he suggested that we may have to examine all instances of mental conflict from the point of view of a struggle between libidinal and destructive impulses.

In discussing his psychoanalytic approach to narcissistic neurosis in 1916 Freud emphasized the impenetrable stone wall which he encountered. However, when in 1937 he described the deep-seated resistances to analytic treatment he did not explicitly relate the resistances in narcissistic conditions to the resistances in states of inertia and in the negative therapeutic reactions, which he did attribute to the death instinct. One of the main reasons for this omission may be that Freud's whole theory of primary narcissism had originally been based on the idea of the individual's directing his libido towards the self and of secondary narcissism being due to a withdrawal of libido from the object back on to the self – and only after he had clarified his ideas on the pleasure principle and the reality principle in 1913, and brought these ideas in relation to love and hate in 'Instincts and their Vicissitudes' (1915) did he begin to feel that there was some important connection between a pleasurable narcissistic stage and hatred or destructiveness towards the external object when the object begins to impinge on the individual. For example, in 1915 he states:

> When during the stage of primary narcissism the object makes its appearance, the second opposite to loving, namely hating, also attains its development.

In the same paper he emphasizes the primary importance of aggression: hate, as a relation to objects, is older than love. It derives from the narcissistic ego's primordial repudiation of the external world with its outpouring stimuli.

Something of the same line of thought can be seen in Freud's view of the Nirvana principle, which he sees as a withdrawal or regression to primary narcissism under the dominance of the death instinct – where peace, an inanimate state and giving in to death are equated.

Hartmann et al. (1949) seemed to have a similar impression of Freud's ideas on the relation of aggression to narcissism when they wrote:

> Freud was used to comparing the relation between narcissism and object love to that between self-destruction and destruction of the object. This analogy might have contributed to his assumption of self-destruction as of the primary form of aggression to be compared with primary narcissism.

From all this it is clear that Freud must have realized the obvious relation between narcissism, narcissistic withdrawal and the death instinct; but he did not work it out in any detail either theoretically or clinically. As I shall go on to show later in this paper, I feel these connections are of considerable clinical significance.

Returning now to the question of the hidden transference in the sense of clinical resistances which Freud (1937) related to the silent opposition of the death instinct, it is important to realize that he thought that these resistances could not be successfully treated by analysis: he apparently believed that the hidden silent aggression of the death instinct could not be analysed unless it emerged as an open negative transference and that interpretations could do nothing to 'activate' it.

Abraham went much further than Freud in studying the hidden negative transference and in clarifying the nature of the destructive impulses which he encountered in his clinical work with narcissistic patients. In psychotic narcissistic patients he stressed the haughty superiority and aloofness of the narcissist and interpreted the negative aggressive attitude in the transference. As early as 1919 he had contributed to the analysis of the hidden negative transference by describing a particular form of neurotic resistance against the analytic method. He found in these patients a most pronounced narcissism, and he emphasized the hostility and defiance hidden behind an apparent eagerness to cooperate. He described how the narcissistic attitude attached itself to the transference and how these patients depreciate and devalue the analyst and grudge him the analytic role representing the father. They reverse the position of patient and analyst to show their superiority over him. He emphasized that the element of envy was unmistakable in these patients' behaviour and in this way clinically and theoretically he connected narcissism and aggression. It is, however, interesting to note that Abraham never attempted to link his findings with Freud's theory of the life and death instincts.

Reich was opposed to Freud's theory of the death instinct. He did, however, make fundamental contributions to the analysis of narcissism and the latent negative transference. He also emphasized, contrary to Freud, that the patient's narcissistic attitudes and latent conflicts, which include negative feelings, could be activated and brought to the surface in analysis and then worked through. He thought that every case without exception begins analysis with a more or less explicit attitude of distrust and criticism which, as a rule, remains hidden.

He considered that the analyst has constantly to point to what is hidden and he should not be misled by an apparent positive transference towards the analyst. Reich studied in detail the character armour where the narcissistic defence finds its concrete chronic expression. In describing the narcissistic patient he stressed their superior, derisive and envious attitude, as well as their contemptuous behaviour. One patient who was constantly preoccupied with thoughts of death complained in every session that the analysis did not touch him and was completely useless. The patient also admitted his boundless envy, not of the analyst, but of other men towards whom he felt inferior. Gradually Reich realized and was able to show the patient his triumph over the analyst, and his attempts to make him feel useless, inferior and impotent so that he could achieve nothing. The patient was then able to admit that he could not tolerate the superiority of anyone and always tried to tear people down. Reich states: 'There then was the patient's suppressed aggression, the most extreme manifestation of which had thus far been his death wishes'. Reich's findings in connection with latent aggression, envy and narcissism have many similarities to Abraham's description of the narcissistic resistance in 1919.

Of the many analysts who have accepted Freud's theory of the interaction between the life and death instincts Melanie Klein's contribution deserves particular consideration as her work is essentially based on this assumption both theoretically and clinically. She also made important contributions to the analysis of the negative transference. She found that envy, particularly in its split-off form, was an important factor in producing chronic negative attitudes in analysis, including 'negative therapeutic reactions'. She described the early infantile mechanisms of splitting the objects and the ego, which enable the infantile ego to keep love and hate apart. In her contributions to narcissism she stressed more the libidinal aspects and suggested that narcissism is in fact a secondary phenomenon which is based on a relationship with an internal good or ideal object, which in fantasy forms part of the loved body and self. She thought that in narcissistic states withdrawal from external relationships to an identification with an idealized internal object takes place.

Melanie Klein wrote in 1958 that she observed in her analytical work with young children a constant struggle between an irrepressible urge to destroy their objects and a desire to preserve them. She felt that Freud's discovery of the life and death instincts was a tremendous advance in understanding this struggle. She believed that anxiety arises from the operation of the death instinct within the organism, which is experienced as a fear of annihilation.

In order to defend itself against this anxiety the primitive ego uses two processes: Part of the death instinct is projected into the external object which hereby becomes a persecutor, while that part of the death instinct, which is retained in the ego, turns its aggression against the persecutory object.

The life instinct is also projected into external objects, which are then felt to be loving or idealized. She emphasizes that it is characteristic for early development that the idealized and the bad persecuting objects are split and kept wide apart, which would imply that the life and death instincts are kept in a state of defusion. Simultaneously with the splitting of the objects the splitting of the self into good and bad parts takes place. These processes of ego splitting also keep the instincts in a state of defusion. Almost simultaneously with the projective processes another primary process, introjection, starts, largely in the service of the life instinct: it combats the death instinct because it leads to the ego taking in something life-giving (first of all food) and thus binding the death instinct working within.

This process is essential in initiating the fusion of the life and death instincts. As the processes of splitting of the object and the self and therefore the states of defusion of the instincts originate in early infancy at a phase which Melanie Klein described as the 'paranoid schizoid position' one may expect the most complete states of defusion of instincts in those clinical conditions where paranoid schizoid mechanisms predominate. We may encounter these states in patients who have never completely outgrown this early phase of development or have regressed to it. Melanie Klein emphasized that early infantile mechanisms and object relations attach themselves to the transference and in this way the processes of splitting the self and objects, which promote the defusion of the instincts, can be investigated and modified in analysis. She also stressed that through investigating these early processes in the transference she became convinced that the analysis of the negative transference was a precondition for analysing the deeper layers of the mind. It was particularly through investigating the negative aspects of the early infantile transference that Melanie Klein came up against primitive envy which she regarded as a direct derivative of the death instinct. She thought that envy appears as a hostile, life-destroying force in the relation of the infant to its mother and is particularly directed against the good feeding mother because she is not only needed by the infant but envied for containing everything which the infant wants to possess himself. In the transference this manifests itself in the patient's need to devalue analytic work which he has found helpful. It appears that envy representing almost completely defused destructive energy is particularly unbearable to the infantile ego and early on in life becomes split off from the rest of the ego. Melanie Klein stressed that split-off, unconscious envy often remained unexpressed in analysis, but nevertheless exerted a troublesome and powerful influence in preventing progress in the analysis, which ultimately can only be effective if it achieves integration and deals with the whole of the personality. In other words the defusion of the instincts has gradually to change to fusion in any successful analysis. Freud's theory of the fusion and defusion of the life and death instincts seems vital for the understanding of defused destructive processes.

Hartmann et al. stressed in 1949 that 'little is known about the fusion and defusion of aggression and libido'. Hartmann himself concentrated on studying the function of neutralized libidinal and aggressive energy, which is probably one of the aspects of the normal fusion of the basic instincts. He also stressed the importance of de-neutralization of libido and aggression in psychotic states such as schizophrenia and stated that defusion and de-neutralization may be interrelated (1953). Freud suggested that defusion of the instincts becomes manifest clinically when regression to earlier phases of development takes place.

I have attempted to clarify the origin of the processes of defusion and fusion of the instincts by relating them to Melanie Klein's theory of the process of splitting of objects and the ego. This splitting is a normal defence mechanism in early life aimed at protecting the self and object from the danger of annihilation by the destructive impulses deriving from the death instinct. This may explain why defusion of the instincts plays an important role in the psychopathology of narcissistic patients and why defused destructive impulses can be observed distinctly in patients emerging from narcissistic states. For this reason I shall concentrate on the examination of the libidinal and destructive aspects of narcissism and shall attempt to clarify in my clinical material how some of the severe defusions of the instincts arise and indicate the factors contributing to normal and pathological fusions.

I introduced the concept of pathological fusion for those processes where in the mixing of libidinal and destructive impulses the power of the destructive impulses is greatly strengthened, while in normal fusion the destructive energy is mitigated or neutralized.

Finally I shall present case material to illustrate the clinical importance of defused and split-off aggression in creating obstacles to analysis, such as chronic resistances and negative therapeutic reactions.

In my previous work on narcissism (1964) I stressed the projective and introjective identification of self and object (fusion of self and object) in narcissistic states, which act as a defence against any recognition of separateness between the self and objects. Awareness of separation immediately leads to feelings of dependence on an object and therefore to inevitable frustrations. However, dependence also stimulates envy, when the goodness of the object is recognized. Aggressiveness towards objects therefore seems inevitable in giving up the narcissistic position and it appears that the strength and persistence of omnipotent narcissistic object relations is closely related to the strength of the envious destructive impulses.

In studying narcissism in greater detail it seems to me essential to differentiate between the libidinal and the destructive aspects of narcissism. In considering narcissism from the libidinal aspect one can see that the overvaluation of the self plays a central role, based mainly on the idealization of the self. Self-idealization is maintained by omnipotent introjective and projective identifications with good objects and their qualities. In this way the narcissist feels that everything that is valuable relating to external objects and the outside world is part of him or is omnipotently controlled by him.

Similarly, when considering narcissism from the destructive aspect, we find that again self-idealization plays a central role, but now it is the idealization of the omnipotent destructive parts of the self. They are directed both against any positive libidinal object relationship and any libidinal part of the self which experiences need for an object and the desire to depend on it. The destructive omnipotent parts of the self often remain disguised or they may be silent and split off, which obscures their existence and gives the impression that they have no relationship to the external world. In fact they have a very powerful effect in preventing dependent object relations and in keeping external objects permanently devalued, which accounts for the apparent indifference of the narcissistic individual towards external objects and the world.

In the narcissism of most patients libidinal and destructive aspects exist side by side but the violence of the destructive impulses varies. In the narcissistic states where the libidinal aspects predominate destructiveness becomes apparent as soon as the omnipotent self-idealization is threatened by contact with an object which is perceived as separate from the self. The patient feels humiliated and defeated by the revelation that it is the external object which, in reality, contains the valuable qualities which he had attributed to his own creative powers. In analysis one observes that when the patient's feelings of resentment and revenge at being robbed of his omnipotent narcissism diminishes, envy is consciously experienced, since it is then that he becomes aware of the analyst as a valuable external person.

When the destructive aspects predominate the envy is more violent and appears as a wish to destroy the analyst as the object who is the real source of life and goodness. At the same time violent self-destructive impulses appear, and these I want to consider in more detail. In terms of the infantile situation the narcissistic patient wants to believe that he has given life to himself and is able to feed and look after himself. When he is faced with the reality of being dependent on the analyst, standing for the parents, particularly the mother, he would prefer to die, to be non-existent, to deny the fact of his birth, and also to destroy his analytic progress and insight representing the child in himself, which he feels the analyst, representing the parents, has created. Frequently at this point the patient wants to give up the analysis but more often he acts out in a self-destructive way by spoiling his professional success and his personal relations. Some of these patients become suicidal and the desire to die, to disappear into oblivion, is expressed quite openly and death is idealized as a solution to all problems.

As the individual seems determined to satisfy a desire to die and to disappear into nothing which resembles Freud's description of the 'pure' death instinct, one might consider that we are dealing in these states with the death instinct in complete defusion. However, analytically one can observe that the state is caused by the activity of destructive envious parts of the self which become severely split off and defused from the libidinal caring self which seems to have disappeared. The whole self becomes temporarily identified with the destructive self, which aims to triumph over life and creativity represented by the parents and the analyst by destroying the dependent libidinal self experienced as the child.

The patient often believes that he has destroyed his caring self, his love, for ever and there is nothing anybody can do to change the situation. When this problem is worked through in the transference and some libidinal part of the patient is experienced as coming alive, concern for the analyst, standing for the mother, appears which mitigates the destructive impulses and lessens the dangerous defusion.

There are some narcissistic patients where defused destructive impulses seem to be constantly active and dominate the whole of their personality and object relations. They express their feelings in an only slightly disguised way by devaluing the analyst's work with their persistent indifference, tricky repetitive behaviour and sometimes open belittlement. In this way they assert their superiority over the analyst representing life and creativity by wasting or destroying his work, understanding and satisfaction. They feel superior in being able to control and withhold those parts of themselves which want to depend on the analyst as a helpful person. They behave as if the loss of any love object including the analyst would leave them cold and even stimulate a feeling of triumph. Such patients occasionally experience shame and some persecutory anxiety but only minimal guilt, because very little of their libidinal self is kept alive. It appears that these patients have dealt with the struggle between their destructive and libidinal impulses by trying to get rid of their concern and love for their objects by killing their loving dependent self and identifying themselves almost entirely with the destructive narcissistic part of the self which provides them with a sense of superiority and self-admiration.

One narcissistic patient, who kept relations to external objects and the analyst dead and empty by constantly deadening any part of his self that attempted object relations, dreamt of a small boy who was in a comatose condition, dying from some kind of poisoning. He was lying on a bed in the courtyard and was endangered by the hot midday sun which was beginning to shine on him. The patient was standing near to the boy but did nothing to move or protect him. He only felt critical and superior to the doctor treating the child, since it was he who should have seen that the child was moved into the shade. The patient's previous behaviour and associations made it clear that the dying boy stood for his dependent libidinal self which he kept in a dying condition by preventing it from getting help and nourishment from the analyst. I showed him that even when he came close to realizing the seriousness of his mental state, experienced as a dying condition, he did not lift a finger to help himself or to help the analyst to make a move towards saving him, because he was using the killing of his infantile dependent self to triumph over the analyst and to show him up as a failure. The dream illustrates clearly that the destructive narcissistic state is maintained in power by keeping the libidinal infantile self in a constant dead or dying condition.

Occasionally the analytic interpretations penetrated the narcissistic shell and the patient felt more alive. He then admitted that he would like to improve but soon he felt his mind drifting away from the consulting room and became so detached and sleepy that he could scarcely keep awake. There was an enormous resistance, almost like a stone wall, which prevented any examination of the situation, but gradually it became clear that the patient felt pulled away from any closer contact with the analyst, because as soon as he felt helped there was not only the danger that he might experience a greater need for the analyst but he feared that he would attack him with sneering and belittling thoughts. Contact with the analyst meant a weakening of the narcissistic omnipotent superiority of the patient and the experience of a conscious feeling of overwhelming envy which was strictly avoided by the detachment.

The destructive narcissism of these patients appears often highly organized, as if one were dealing with a powerful gang dominated by a leader, who controls all the members of the gang to see that they support one another in making the criminal destructive work more effective and powerful. However, the narcissistic organization not only increases the strength of the destructive narcissism, but it has a defensive purpose to keep itself in power and so maintain the status quo. The main aim seems to be to prevent the weakening of the organization and to control the members of the gang so that they will not desert the destructive organization and join the positive parts of the self or betray the secrets of the gang to the police, the protecting superego, standing for the helpful analyst, who might be able to save the patient. Frequently when a patient of this kind makes progress in the analysis and wants to change he dreams of being attacked by members of the Mafia or adolescent delinquents and a negative therapeutic reaction sets in. This narcissistic organization is in my experience not primarily directed against guilt and anxiety, but seems to have the purpose of maintaining the idealization and superior power of the destructive narcissism. To change, to receive help, implies weakness and is experienced as wrong or as failure by the destructive narcissistic organization which provides the patient with his sense of superiority. In cases of this kind there is a most determined chronic resistance to analysis and only the very detailed exposure of the system enables analysis to make some progress.

In many of these patients the destructive impulses are linked with perversions. In this situation the apparent fusion of the instincts does not lead to a lessening of the power of the destructive instincts; on the contrary the power and violence is greatly increased through the erotization of the aggressive instinct. I feel it is confusing to follow Freud in discussing perversions as fusions between the life and death instincts because in these instances the destructive part of the self has taken control over the whole of the libidinal aspects of the patient's personality and is therefore able to misuse them. These cases are in reality instances of pathological fusion similar to the confusional states where the destructive impulses overpower the libidinal ones.

In some narcissistic patients the destructive narcissistic parts of the self are linked to a psychotic structure or organization which is split off from the rest of the personality. This psychotic structure is like a delusional world or object, into which parts of the self tend to withdraw. It appears to be dominated by an omnipotent or omniscient extremely ruthless part of the self, which creates the notion that within the delusional object there is complete painlessness but also freedom to indulge in any sadistic activity. The whole structure is committed to narcissistic self-sufficiency and is strictly directed against any object relatedness. The destructive impulses within this delusional world sometimes appear openly as overpoweringly cruel, threatening the rest of the self with death to assert their power, but more frequently they appear disguised as omnipotently benevolent or life-saving, promising to provide the patient with quick, ideal solutions to all his problems. These false promises are designed to make the normal self of the patient dependent on or addicted to his omnipotent self, and to lure the normal sane parts into this delusional structure in order to imprison them. When narcissistic patients of this type begin to make some progress and to form some dependent relationship to the analysis, severe negative thera-peutic reactions occur as the narcissistic psychotic part of the self exerts its power and superiority over life and the analyst, standing for reality, by trying to lure the dependent self into a psychotic omnipotent dream state which results in the patient losing his sense of reality and his capacity for thinking. In fact there is a danger of an acute psychotic state if the dependent part of the patient, which is the sanest part of his personality, is persuaded to turn away from the external world and give itself up entirely to the domination of the psychotic delusional structure. This process has similarities to Freud's description of the giving up of object cathexis and the withdrawal of the libido into the ego. The state I am describing implies the withdrawal of the self away from libidinal object cathexis into a narcissistic state which resembles primary narcissism. The patient appears to be withdrawn from the world, is unable to think and often feels drugged. He may lose his interest in the outside world and want to stay in bed and forget what had been discussed in previous sessions. If he manages to come to the session, he may complain that something incomprehensible has happened to him and that he feels trapped, claustrophobic and unable to get out of this state. He is often aware that he has lost something important but is not sure what it is. The loss may be felt in concrete terms as a loss of his keys or his wallet, but sometimes he realizes that his anxiety and feeling of loss refers to having lost an important part of himself, namely the sane dependent self which is related to the capacity for thinking. Sometimes the patient develops an acute hypochondriacal fear of death which is quite overwhelming. One has here the impression of being able to observe the death instinct in its purest form, as a power which manages to pull the whole of the self away from life into a deathlike condition by false promises of a Nirvana-like state, which would imply a complete defusion of the basic instincts. However, detailed investigation of the process suggests that we are not dealing with a state of defusion but a pathological fusion similar to the process I described in the perversions. In this narcissistic withdrawal state the sane dependent part of the patient enters the delusional object and a projective identification takes place in which the sane self loses its identity and becomes completely dominated by the omnipotent destructive process; it has no power to oppose or mitigate the latter while this pathological fusion lasts; on the contrary, the power of the destructive process is greatly increased in this situation.

Clinically it is essential to help the patient to find and rescue the dependent sane part of the self from its trapped position inside the psychotic narcissistic structure as it is this part which is the essential link with the positive object relationship to the analyst and the world. Secondly, it is important gradually to assist the patient to become fully conscious of the split-off destructive omnipotent parts of the self which control the psychotic organization, because this can only remain all-powerful in isolation. When this process is fully revealed it becomes clear that it contains the destructive envious impulses of the self which have become isolated and then the omnipotence which has such a hypnotic effect on the whole of the self gets deflated and the infantile nature of the omnipotence can be exposed. In other words, the patient becomes gradually aware that he is dominated by an omnipotent infantile part of himself which not only pulls him away towards death but infantilizes him and prevents him from growing up, by keeping him away from objects who could help him to achieve growth and development.

I shall now briefly report some case material from a narcissistic neurotic patient to illustrate the existence of a split-off, omnipotent, destructive part of himself which became more conscious during analysis and lost some of its violence. The patient is an unmarried business man of 37, who has been in treatment for several years. He came to analysis because of character problems and was consciously very determined to have analysis and to cooperate in it. However, there was a chronic resistance to the analysis, which was very elusive and repetitive. The patient had to leave London occasionally for short business trips and he often returned too late on Mondays and so missed either part or the whole of his session. He frequently met women during these trips and brought to analysis many of the problems which arose with them. It was, of course, clear from the beginning that some acting out was taking place but only when he regularly reported murderous activities in his dreams after such weekends did it become apparent that violently destructive attacks against the analysis and the analyst were hidden in the acting out behaviour. The patient was at first reluctant to accept that the acting out of the weekend was killing, and therefore blocking the progress of, the analysis, but gradually he changed his behaviour and the analysis became more effective and he reported considerable improvement in some of his personal relationships and his business activities. At the same time he began to complain that his sleep was frequently disturbed and that he woke up during the night with violent palpitations which kept him awake for several hours. During these anxiety attacks he felt that his hands did not belong to him; they seemed violently destructive as if they wanted to destroy something by tearing it up, and were too powerful for him to control so that he had to give in to them. He then dreamt of a very powerful arrogant man who was nine feet tall and who insisted that he had to be absolutely obeyed. His associations made it clear that this man stood for a part of himself and related to the destructive overpowering feelings in his hands which he could not resist. I interpreted that he regarded the omnipotent destructive part of himself as a superman who was nine feet tall and much too powerful for him to disobey. He had disowned this omnipotent self, which explained the estrangement of his hands during the nightly attacks. I further explained this split-off self as an infantile omnipotent part which claimed that it was not an infant but stronger and more powerful than all the adults, particularly his mother and father and now the analyst. His adult self was so completely taken in and therefore weakened by this omnipotent assertion that he felt powerless to fight the destructive impulses at night. The patient reacted to the inter- pretation with surprise and relief and reported after some days that he felt more able to control his hands at night. He became gradually more aware that the destructive impulses at night had some connection with analysis because they increased after any success which could be attributed to it. Thus he saw that the wish to tear at himself was related to a wish to tear out and destroy a part of himself which depended on the analyst and valued him. Simultaneously the aggressive narcissistic impulses which had been split off became more conscious during analytic sessions and he sneered saying: 'Here you have to sit all day wasting your time'. He felt that he was the important person and he should be free to do anything he wanted to do, however cruel and hurting this might be to others and himself. He was particularly enraged by the insight and understanding which the analysis gave him. He hinted that his rage was related to wanting to reproach me for helping him, because this interfered with his omnipotent acting-out beha- viour. He then reported a dream, that he was running a long-distance race and he was working very hard at it. However, there was a young woman who did not believe in anything that he was doing. She was unprincipled, nasty and did everything to interfere and mislead him. There was a refer- ence to the woman's brother, who was called 'Mundy'. He was much more aggressive than his sister and he appeared in the dream snarling like a wild beast, even at her. It was reported in the dream that this brother had had the task of misleading everybody, during the previous year. The patient thought that the name 'Mundy' referred to his frequent missing of the Monday sessions a year ago. He realized that the violent uncontrolled aggressiveness related to himself but he felt the young woman was also himself. During the last year he had often insisted in his analytic sessions that he felt he was a woman, and was very contemptuous of and superior to the analyst. Lately, however, he occasionally dreamt of a little girl who was receptive and appreciative of her teachers, which I had interpreted as a part of him which wanted to show more appreciation of the analyst, but was prevented from coming into the open by his omnipotence. In the dream the patient admits that the aggressive omnipotent part of himself, represented as male, which had dominated the acting out until a year ago, had now become quite conscious. His identification with the analyst is expressed in the dream as a determination to work hard at his analysis. The dream, however, is also a warning that he would continue his aggressive acting out in analysis by asserting in a misleading way that he could present himself omnipotently as a grown-up woman instead of allowing himself to respond to the work of the analysis with receptive feelings relating to a more positive infantile part of himself. In fact the patient was moving in the analysis towards a strengthening of his positive dependence, which enabled him to expose openly the opposition of the aggressive narcissistic omnipotent parts of his personality; in other words, the patient's severe instinctual defusion is gradually developing into normal fusion.

SUMMARY

I have attempted in this paper to investigate clinical conditions where aggressive impulses predominate and examine their relation to Freud's theory of the defusion and fusion of the life and death instincts. I have found that even in the most severe states of defusion of the instincts clinical states which resemble Freud's description of the death instinct in its original form reveal on detailed analysis that it is the destructive aspect of the death instinct which is active in paralysing, or psychically killing, the libidinal parts of the self derived from the life instinct. I therefore think that it is not possible to observe an unfused death instinct in the clinical situation.

Some of these destructive states cannot be described as defusions because they are really pathological fusions, in which the psychic structure dominated by a destructive part of the self succeeds in imprisoning and overpowering the libidinal self, which is completely unable to oppose the destructive process.

It seems that certain omnipotent, narcissistic states are dominated by the most violent destructive processes, so that the libidinal self is almost completely absent or lost. Clinically it is therefore essential to find access to the libidinal dependent self, which can mitigate the destructive impulses. In analysing the omnipotent structure of the narcissistic state the infantile nature of the process has to be exposed in order to release these dependent parts which can form good object relations leading to the introjection of libidinal objects which are the basis of normal fusion.

References

Abraham, K. (1919) 'A Particular Form of Neurotic Resistance Against the Psychoanalytic Method', in *Selected Papers* (1942), London: Hogarth Press.

Abraham, K. (1924) 'A Short Study of the Development of the Libido Viewed in the Light of Mental Disorders', in *Selected Papers* (1942), London: Hogarth Press.

Freud, S. (1913) 'Formulations on the Two Principles of Mental Functioning', in *SE*, vol. 12.

Freud, S. (1914) 'On Narcissism: An Introduction', in *SE*, vol. 14.

Freud, S. (1915) 'Instincts and Their Vicissitudes', in *SE*, vol. 14.

Freud, S. (1916–17) Introductory Lectures on Psycho-analysis', in *SE*, vols 15–16.

Freud, S. (1920) 'Beyond the Pleasure Principle', in *SE*, vol. 18.

Freud, S. (1923) 'The Ego and the Id', *SE*, vol. 19.

Freud, S. (1924) 'The Economic Problem of Masochism', in *SE*, vol. 19.

Freud, S. (1933) 'New Introductory Lectures on Psycho-analysis', in *SE*, vol. 22.

Freud, S. (1937) 'Analysis Terminable and Interminable', in *SE*, vol. 23.

Hartmann, H. (1953) 'Contribution to the Metapsychology of Schizophrenia', in *Essays on Ego Psychology* (1964), London: Hogarth Press.

Hartmann, H., Kris, E. and Loewenstein, R. M. (1949) 'Notes on the Theory of Aggression', in *Psychoanalytic Study of the Child*, 3–4.

Kernberg, O. F. (1970) 'Factors in the Psychoanalytic Treatment of Narcissistic Personalities', in *Journal of the American Psychoanalytic Association*, vol. 18, 51–85.

Klein M. (1946) 'Notes on Some Schizoid Mechanisms', in *Developments in Psycho-Analysis* (1952), London: Hogarth Press.

Klein, M. (1952) 'The Origins of Transference', in *International Journal of Psycho-analysis*, vol. 33, 433–8.

Klein, M. (1957) *Envy and Gratitude*, London: Tavistock; New York: Basic Books.

Klein, M. (1958) 'On the Development of Mental Functioning', in *International Journal of Psychoanalysis*, vol. 39, 84–90.

Reich, W. (1933) *Character-Analysis* (1949), New York: Orgone Institute Press, 1949.

Rosenfeld, H. (1964) 'On the Psychopathology of Narcissism', in *Psychotic States* (1965), London: Hogarth Press.

Rosenfeld, H. (1968) 'Notes on the Negative Therapeutic Reaction', Paper read to British Psycho-Analytical Society and Menninger Clinic, Topeka.

Rosenfeld, H. (1970) 'On Projective Identification', Paper read to British Psycho-Analytical Society.

Chapter 10

Contribution to the psychopathology of psychotic states: the importance of projective identification in the ego structure and the object relations of the psychotic patient[1][¶]

Herbert A. Rosenfeld

Following the suggestion of the organizers of the Symposium that I should discuss the importance of projective identification and ego splitting in the psychopathology of the psychotic patient, I shall attempt to give you a survey of the processes described under the term: 'projective identification'.

I shall first define the meaning of the term 'projective identification' and quote from the work of Melanie Klein, as it was she who developed the concept. Then I shall go on to discuss very briefly the work of two other writers whose use appeared to be related to, but not identical with, Melanie Klein's use of the term.

'Projective identification' relates first of all to a splitting process of the early ego, where either good or bad parts of the self are split off from the ego and are as a further step projected in love or hatred into external objects which leads to fusion and identification of the projected parts of the self with the external objects. There are important paranoid anxieties related to these processes as the objects filled with aggressive parts of the self become persecuting and are experienced by the patient as threatening to retaliate by forcing themselves and the bad parts of the self which they contain back again into the ego.

In her paper on schizoid mechanisms Melanie Klein (1946) considers first of all the importance of the processes of splitting and denial and omnipotence which during the early phase of development play a role similar to that of repression at a later stage of ego development. She then discusses the early infantile instinctual impulses and suggests that while the 'oral libido still has the lead, libidinal and aggressive impulses and phantasies from other sources come to the fore and lead to a confluence of oral, urethral and anal desires, both libidinal and aggressive'. After discussing

1 This article was first published in 1971 in P. Doucet and C. Laurin (eds) Problems of Psychosis, The Hague: Excerpta Medica, 115–28.
¶ Reprinted with permission from Angela Rosenfeld, Executor for the work of Dr H. A. Rosenfeld.

the oral libidinal and aggressive impulses directed against the breast and the mother's body, she suggests that:

> the other line of attack derives from the anal and urethral impulses and implies expelling dangerous substances (excrements) out of the self and into the mother. Together with these harmful excrements, expelled in hatred, split off parts of the ego are also projected into the mother. These excrements and bad parts of the self are meant not only to injure but also to control and to take possession of the object. In so far as the mother comes to contain the bad parts of the self, she is not felt to be a separate individual but is felt to be the bad self. Much of the hatred against parts of the self is now directed towards the mother. This leads to a particular form of identification which establishes the prototype of an aggressive object relation. I suggest for these process to term *projective identification*.

Later on in the same paper Melanie Klein describes that not only bad, but also good parts of the ego are expelled and projected into external objects who become identified with the projected good parts of the self. She regards this identification as vital because it is essential for the infant's ability to develop good object relations. If this process is, however, excessive, good parts of the personality are felt to be lost to the self which results in weakening and impoverishment of the ego. Melanie Klein also emphasizes the aspect of the projective processes which relates to the forceful entry into the object and the persecutory anxieties related to this process which I mentioned before. She also describes how paranoid anxieties related to projective identification disturb introjective processes. 'Introjection is interfered with, as it may be felt as a forceful entry from the outside into the inside in retribution for violent projections.' It will be clear that Melanie Klein gives the name 'projective identification' both to the processes of ego splitting and the 'narcissistic' object relations created by the projection of parts of the self into objects.

I shall now discuss some aspects of the work of Dr Edith Jacobson who describes psychotic identifications in schizophrenic patients identical with the ones I observed and descried as 'projective identification'. She also frequently uses the term 'projective identification' in her book *Psychotic Conflict and Reality* (Jacobson 1967).

In 1954 Edith Jacobson discussed the identifications of the delusional schizophrenic patient who may eventually consciously believe himself to be another person. She relates this to early infantile identification mechanisms of a magic nature which lead to 'partial or total blending of the magic self and object images, founded on phantasies or even the temporary belief of being one with or of becoming the object, regardless of reality'. In 1967 she describes these processes in more detail. She discusses 'the psychotic's regression to a narcissistic level, where the weakness of the boundaries between self and object images gives rise to phantasies, or experiences of fusion between these images. These primitive introjective or projective identifications are based on infantile phantasies of incorporation, devouring, invading (forcing oneself into), or being devoured by the object.' She also says 'We can assume that such phantasies, which pre-suppose at least the beginning distinction between self and object, are characteristic of early narcissistic stages of development and that the child's relation to the mother normally begins with the introjective and projective processes'; and that the 'introjective and projective identifications (of the adult patient) depend on the patient's fixation to early narcissistic stages and upon the depth of the narcissistic regression'. In discussing clinical material of the Patient A she described this fear that any affectionate physical contact might bring about experiences of merging, which in turn might lead to a manifest psychotic state. Her views that the introjective and projective identifications observed in the adult patient depend on the fixation to early narcissistic phases where these identifications originate, seem identical with my own views and there is nothing in her clinical and theoretical observations which I have quoted above with which I would disagree. She stresses, however, that she differs from Melanie Klein and my own opinion in so far as she does not believe that the projective identifications of the adult patient observable in the transference or acted out by the patient with objects in his environment are in fact a repetition of the early infantile projective and introjective processes, but are to be understood as a later defensive process, as in her view early processes cannot be observed in the transference. She also disagrees with my analytic technique of verbally interpreting the processes of projective identification when they appear in the transference, which I regard as of central importance in working through psychotic processes in the transference situation.[1]

Margaret Mahler in 1952 described symbiotic infantile psychoses and suggested that the mechanisms employed are introjective and projective ones and their psychotic elaboration. Her ideas seem to be closely related, but nevertheless quite distinct from what I have described as projective identification. She describes the early mother–infant relationship as a phase of object relationship in which the infant behaves and functions as though he and his mother were an omnipotent system (a dual unity with one common boundary, a symbiotic membrane as it were). In 1967 she says, 'the essential feature of symbiosis is hallucinatory or delusional, somatopsychic, omnipotent fusion with the representation of the mother and, in particular, delusion of common boundary of the two actually and physically separate individuals'. She suggests that 'this is the mechanism to which the ego regresses in cases of psychotic disorganization'. In describing the symbiotic infantile psychosis she says that the early mother–infant symbiotic relationship is intense. The mental representation of the mother remains or is regressively fused with that of the self. She describes the panic reactions caused by separations 'which are followed by restitutive productions which serve to maintain or restore the symbiotic parasitic delusion of oneness with the mother or father'. It is clear that Mahler has introjective or projective processes in mind as the mechanisms which produce the symbiotic psychosis. I have, however, found no clear description of these mechanisms in her papers. She seems to see the symbiotic psychosis as a defence against separation anxiety which links up closely with my description of the narcissistic object relation serving a defensive function. The symbiotic processes described by Mahler have some resemblance to the parasitical object relations I shall describe later. Projective identification which includes ego splitting and projecting of good and bad parts of the self into external objects is not identical with symbiosis. For projective identification to take place some temporary differentiation of 'me' and 'not me' is essential. Symbiosis, however, is used by Mahler to describe this state of undifferentiation, of fusion with the mother, in which the 'I' is not yet differentiated from the 'not I'.

In my own work with psychotic patients I have encountered a variety of types of object relations and mental mechanisms which are associated with Melanie Klein's description of projective identification. First of all, it is important to distinguish between two types of projective identification, namely, projective identification used for communication with other objects and projective identification used for ridding the self of unwanted parts.

I shall first discuss projective identification used as a method of communication. Many psychotic patients use projective processes for communication with other people. These projective mechanisms of the psychotic seem to be a distortion or intensification of the normal infantile relationship, which is based on non-verbal communication between infant and mother, in which impulses, parts of the self and anxieties too difficult for the infant to bear are projected into the mother and where the mother is able instinctively to respond by containing the infant's anxiety and alleviating it by her behaviour. This relationship has been stressed particularly by Bion. The psychotic patient who uses this process in the transference may do so consciously but more often unconsciously. He then projects impulses and parts of himself into the analyst in order that the analyst will feel and understand his experiences and will be able to contain them so that they lose their frightening or unbearable quality and become meaningful by the analyst being able to put them into words through interpretations. This situation seems to be of fundamental importance for the development of introjective processes and the development of the ego; it makes it possible for the patient to learn to tolerate his own impulses and the analyst's interpretations make his infantile responses and feelings accessible to the more sane self, which can begin to think about the experiences which were previously meaningless and frightening to him. The psychotic patient who projects predominantly for communication is obviously receptive to the analyst's understanding of him, so it is essential that this type of communication should be recognized and interpreted accordingly.

As a second point I want to discuss projective identification used for denial of psychic reality. In this situation the patient splits off parts of his self in addition to impulses and anxieties and projects them into the analyst for the purpose of evacuating and emptying out the disturbing mental content which leads to a denial of psychic reality. As this type of patient primarily wants the analyst to condone the evacuation processes and the denial of his problems, he often reacts to interpretations with violent resentment, as they are experienced as critical and frightening since the patient believes that unwanted unbearable and meaningless mental content is pushed back into him by the analyst.

Both the processes of communication and evacuation may exist simultaneously or alternatively in our psychotic patients and it is essential to differentiate them clearly in order to keep contact with the patient and make analysis possible.

As a third point I want to discuss a very common transference relationship of the psychotic patient which is aimed at controlling the analyst's body and mind, which seems to be based on a very early infantile type of object relationship.

In analysis, one observes that the patient believes that he has forced himself omnipotently into the analyst, which leads to fusion or confusion with the analyst and anxieties relating to the loss of the self. In this form of projective identification the projection of the mad parts of the self into the analyst often predominates. The analyst is then perceived as having become mad, which arouses extreme anxiety as the patient is afraid that the analyst will retaliate and force the madness back into the patient, depriving him entirely of his sanity. At such times the patient is in danger of disintegration, but detailed interpretations of the relationship between patient and analyst may break through this omnipotent delusional situation and prevent a breakdown.

There is, however, a danger that the verbal communication between patient and analyst may break down at such times as the analyst's interpretations are misunderstood and misinterpreted by the patient and the patient's communications increasingly assume a concrete quality, suggesting that abstract thinking has almost completely broken down. In investigating such situations, I found that omnipotent projective identification interferes with the capacity of verbal and abstract thinking and produces a concreteness of the mental processes which leads to confusion between reality and phantasy. It is also clinically essential for the analyst to realize that the patient who uses excessive projective identification is dominated by concrete thought processes which cause misunderstanding of verbal interpretations, since words and their content are experienced by the patient as concrete, non-symbolic objects. Segal in her paper 'Some Aspects of the Analysis of a Schizophrenic' (1950) points out that the schizophrenic patient loses the capacity to use symbols when the symbol becomes again the equivalent of the original objects, which means it is hardly different from it. In her paper 'Notes on Symbol Formation' (1957) she suggest the term 'symbolic equation' for this process: she writes:

> The symbolic equation between the original object and the symbol in the internal and external world is, I think, the basis of the schizo-phrenic's concrete thinking. This non-differentiation between the thing symbolized and the symbol is part of a disturbance in the relation between the ego and the object. Parts of the ego and internal objects are projected onto an object and identified with it. The differentiation between the self and the object is obscured then; since a part of the ego is confused with the object, the symbol which is a creation and a function of the ego becomes in turn confused with the object which is symbolized.

I believe that the differentiation of the self and object representation is necessary to maintain normal symbol formation which is based on the introjection of objects experienced as separate from the self.[2] It is the excessive projective identification in the psychotic process which obliterates differentiation of self and objects, which causes confusion between reality and phantasy and a regression to concrete thinking due to the loss of the capacity for symbolisation and symbolic thinking.[3]

It is, of course, extremely difficult to use verbal interpretations with the psychotic patient when interpretations are misunderstood and misinter-preted. The patient may become extremely frightened, may cover his ears and try to rush out of the consulting room and the analysis is in danger of breaking down. At such times it is necessary to uncover the projective processes used for the purpose of communication between patient and analyst, which will establish some possibility of simple verbal interpreta-tions to explain to the patient and help him to understand the terrifying situation due to the concrete experience. It is essential for the analyst to remember that all three types of projective identification which I have described so far exist simultaneously in the psychotic patient, and one-sided concentration on one process may block the analysis and meaningful communication between patient and analyst.

There is one further aspect of the psychopathology of psychotic patients that is linked with projective identification – that is the importance of primitive aggression, particularly envy, and the use of projective identi-fication to deal with it.

When the psychotic patient living in a state of fusion (projective identi-fication) with the analyst begins to experience himself as a separate person, violent destructive impulses make their appearance. His aggressive impulses are sometimes an expression of anger related to separation anxiety, but generally they have a distinctly envious character. As long as the patient regards the analyst's mind and body and his help and understanding as part of his own self he is able to attribute everything that is experienced as valuable in the analysis as being part of his own self, in other words he lives in a state of omnipotent narcissism. As soon as a patient begins to feel separate from the analyst the aggressive reaction appears and particularly clearly so after a valuable interpretation, which shows the analyst's understanding. The patient reacts with feelings of humiliation, complains that he is made to feel small; why should the analyst be able to remind him of something which he needs but which he cannot provide for himself. In his envious anger the patient tries to destroy and spoil the analyst's interpretations by ridiculing or making them meaningless. The analyst may have the distinct experience in his counter transference that he is meant to feel that he is no good and has nothing of value to give to the patient. There are often physical symptoms connected with this state because the patient may feel sick and may actually vomit. This concrete rejection of the analyst's help can often be clearly understood as a rejection of the mother's food[4] and her care for the infant repeated in the analytic transference situation. When the patient had previously made good progress in the treatment this 'negative therapeutic reaction' is often quite violent, as if he wants to spoil and devalue everything he had previously received, disregarding the often suicidal danger of such a reaction. Many patients experience this violent envy directed against the good qualities of the analyst as quite insane and illogical and as the inner saner part of the patient experiences these envious reactions as unbearable and unacceptable, many defences against this primitive envy are created.

One of these defences relates to the splitting off and projection of the envious part of the self into an external object, which then becomes the envious part of the patient. This kind of defensive projective identification follows the model of Melanie Klein's description of the splitting off and projection of bad parts of the self, which I quoted in the beginning of this paper.

Another defence against envy relates to omnipotent phantasies of the patient of entering the admired and envied object and in this way insisting that he is the object by taking over its role. When total projective identification has taken place with an envied object envy is entirely denied, but immediately reappears when the self and object become separate again. In my paper on 'The Psychopathology of Narcissism' (1964) I stressed that:

> projective identification was part of an early narcissistic relationship to the mother, where recognition of separateness between self and object is denied. Awareness of separation would lead to feelings of dependence

on an object and therefore to anxiety (see Mahler 1967). In addition, dependence stimulates envy when the goodness of the object is recognized. The omnipotent narcissistic object relations, particularly omnipotent projective identification, obviate both the aggressive feelings caused by frustration and any awareness of envy.

I believe that in the psychotic patient projective identification is more often a defence against excessive envy, which is closely bound up with the patient's narcissism, rather than a defence against separation anxiety. In my paper 'Object Relations of an Acute Schizophrenic Patient in the Transference Situation' (1964) I tried to trace the origin of the envious projective identification in schizophrenia. I suggested:

> If too much resentment and envy dominates the infant's relation to the mother, normal projective identification becomes more and more controlling and can take on omnipotent delusional tones. For example, the infant who is phantasy enters the mother's body driven by envy and omnipotence, takes over the role of the mother, or breast, and deludes himself that he is the mother of breast. This mechanism plays an important role in mania and hypomania, but in schizophrenia it occurs in a very exaggerated form.

Finally, I want to draw attention to two similar types of object relations: a parasitical and a delusional one. In the parasitical object relation the psychotic patient in analysis maintains a belief that he is living entirely inside an object – the analyst – and behaves like a parasite living on the capacities of the analyst, who is expected to function as his ego. Severe parasitism may be regarded as a state of total projective identification. It is, however, not just a defensive state to deny envy or separation but is also an expression of aggression, particularly envy. It is the combination of defence and acting out of the aggression which makes the parasitic state a particularly difficult therapeutic problem.

The parasitic patient relies entirely on the analyst, often making him responsible for his entire life. He generally behaves in an extremely passive, silent and sluggish manner, demanding everything and giving nothing in return. This state can be extremely chronic and the analytic work with such patients is often minimal. One of my depressed patients described himself as a baby, which was like a stone heavily pressing into my couch and into me. He felt he was making it impossible for me either to carry him or to look after him and he feared that the only thing that I could possibly do was to expel him, if I could not stand him any longer. However, he was terrified that he could not survive being left. He not only felt that he had a very paralysing effect on the analysis but that he was paralysed and inert himself. Only very occasionally was it possible to get in touch with the intense feelings either of hostility or overwhelming pain and depression bound up with this process. There was not joy when the analyst was felt to be helpful and alive, as it only increased the patient's awareness of the contrast between himself and the analyst and at times produced a desire to frustrate him, and with this he returned to the *status quo* of inertia, which was felt to be unpleasant but preferred to any of the intense feelings of pain, anger, envy or jealousy which might fleetingly be experienced. As I suggested before, extreme parasitism is partly a defence against separation anxiety, envy or jealousy, but it often seems to be a defence against any emotion which might be experienced as painful. I often have the impression that patients, like the one I descried, who experience themselves as dead and are often experienced by the analyst as so inactive that they might as well be dead, use their analyst's aliveness as a means of survival. However, the latent hostility prevents the patient from getting more than minimal help or satisfaction from the analysis. In the more active forms of parasitism the insidious hostility dominates the picture and is much more apparent.

Dr Bion in his book *Transformations* (1965) describes a more active case of parasitism. He emphasizes that such patients are particularly unrewarding. The essential feature is simultaneous stimulation and frustration of hope and work that is fruitless, except for discrediting analyst and patient. The destructive activity is balanced by enough success to deny the patient fulfilment of his destructiveness. 'The helpful summary of such a case is described as "chronic murder of patient and analyst" or "an instance of parasitism": the patient draws on the love, or benevolence of the host to extract knowledge and power which enables him to poison the association and destroy the indulgence on which he depends for his existence.'

It is important to differentiate the very chronic forms of parasitism from the massive intrusion and projective identification into the analyst which resembles parasitism but is of shorter duration and responds more easily to interpretations. It occurs at times when separation threatens or when jealousy or envy is violently stimulated in the transference or in outside life. Meltzer (1967) describes a primitive form of possessive jealousy which plays an important role in perpetuating massive projective identification of a peculiar withdrawn, sleepy sort.

The other form of living entirely inside an object occurs in severely deluded schizophrenic patients who seem to experience themselves as living in an unreal world, which is highly delusional but nevertheless has qualities of a structure which suggests that this hallucinatory world represents the inside of an object, probably the mother. The patient may be withdrawn, preoccupied with hallucinations, in the analysis occasionally projecting the hallucinatory experience on to the analyst, which leads to mis-identifying him and others with his delusional experience. Sometimes the patient may describe himself as living in a world, or object, which separates him entirely from the outside world and the analyst is experienced as a contraption, an actor or a machine and the world becomes extremely unreal. The living inside the delusional object seems to be definitely in opposition to relating to the outside world, which would imply depending on a real object. This delusional world or object seems to be dominated by an omnipotent and sometimes omniscient part of the self, which creates the notion that within the delusional object there is complete painlessness and freedom to indulge in any whim. It also appears that the self within the delusional object exerts a powerful suggestive and seductive influence on saner parts of the personality in order to persuade or force them to withdraw from reality and to join the delusional omnipotent world. Clinically, the patient may hear a voice making propaganda for living inside the mad world by idealizing it and praising its virtue by offering a complete satisfaction and instant cure to the patient. This persuasion or propaganda to get inside the delusional world implies clinically the constant stimulus to all parts of the self to use omnipotent projective identification (forcing the self inside the object) as the only possible method to solve all problems. This situation leads to constant acting out with external objects which are used for projective identification. When, however, projective identification becomes directed towards the delusional object, the saner parts of the self may become trapped or imprisoned within this object and physical and mental paralysis amounting to catatonia may result.

THE PSYCHOANALYTIC TREATMENT OF THE PROCESSES RELATED TO PROJECTIVE IDENTIFICATION IN THE PSYCHOTIC PATIENT

As this paper deals primarily with the psychopathology of psychotic states, I can only briefly discuss my psychoanalytic technique in dealing with psychotic patients to emphasize my contention that the investigation of the psychopathology of the psychotic and the therapeutic approach are closely interlinked.

In treating psychotic states it is absolutely essential to differentiate those parts of the self which exist almost exclusively in a state of projective identification with external objects, or internal ones such as the delusional object I described above and the saner parts of the patient which are less dominated by projective identification and have formed some separate existence from objects. These saner parts may be remnants of the adult personality, but often they represent more normal non-omnipotent infantile parts of the self, which during analysis are attempting to form a dependent relationship to the analyst representing the feeding mother. As the saner parts of the self are in danger of submitting to the persuasion of the delusional self to withdraw into the more psychotic parts of the personality, and to get entangled in it, the former need very careful attention in analysis to help them to differentiate the analyst as an external object from the seductive voice of the omnipotent parts of the self related to the internal delusional object, which can assume any identity for the purpose of keeping up the domination of the whole self. As there is always a conflict, amounting sometimes to a violent struggle between the psychotic and saner parts of the personality, the nature of this conflict has also to be clearly understood in order to make it possible to work through the psychotic state by means of analysis. For example, the structure and the intentions of the psychotic parts of the patient, which are highly narcissistically organized, have to be brought fully into the open by means of interpretations, as they are opposed to any part of the self which wants to form a relationship to reality and to the analyst who attempts to help the ego to move towards growth and development. The interpretations have also to expose the extent and the method used by the psychotic narcissistic parts of the personality in attempting to dominate, entangle and to paralyse the saner parts of the self. It is important to remember that it is only the sane dependent parts of the self separate from the analyst that can use introjective processes uncontaminated by the concreteness caused by the omnipotent projective identifications; the capacity for memory and growth of the ego depends on these normal introjective processes. When the dependent non-psychotic parts of the personality become stronger, as the result of analysis, violent negative therapeutic reactions usually occur as the psychotic narcissistic parts of the patient oppose any progress and change of the *status quo*, a problem which I recently discussed in detail in a paper on 'The Negative Therapeutic Reaction' (Rosenfeld 1969).

CASE PRESENTATION

I shall now bring some case material of a schizophrenic patient in order to illustrate some aspects of projective identification and ego splitting.

Patient A

Had been diagnosed several years ago as schizophrenic, when he had an acute psychotic breakdown which was characterized by overwhelming panic, confusion and fears of complete disintegration. He did not hallucinate during the acute phase, nor are the delusional aspects of the psychosis dominant at the present time, but he is unable to work or to maintain a close relationship with men or women in the outside world. He had been treated by another analyst for several years before starting analysis with me more than a year ago. The previous analyst in his report to me emphasized the patient's tendency to slip into a state of projective identification with the analyst at the beginning of each session leading to the patient becoming confused and unable to speak in an audible and understandable way. The analyst interpreted to the patient that he expected him, the analyst, to understand him even if he could not talk or think, since he believed himself to be inside the analyst; as a result of such interpretations he generally started to speak more distinctly. During the analysis with me there were further improvements and he felt at times more separate, so that the saner parts of his self were able to form to some extent a dependent relationship to me. However, from time to time, particularly after he had made some progress, or when there were long separations, he fell back to a parasitical relationship of living inside me (projective identification) which led to states of confusion, inability to think and talk, claustrophobia and paranoid anxieties of being trapped by me. When envy was aroused through experiences in the real world, for example when he met a man who was successful in his relationship with women or in his work, after a short conscious experience of envy A would frequently become identified with him. This was followed by severe anxieties of losing his identity and feelings of being trapped, rather than leading to the delusion that he was the envied man or that he was able to function in the outside world similarly to the man with whom projective identification and confusion had taken place.

Last year, in the autumn, I had to interrupt the patient's analysis for a fortnight which disturbed him considerably. Consciously, he seem unconcerned about my going away which I had of course discussed with him several months before. However, two weeks before the interruption he became acutely anxious and confused and for a day he feared that he would have another breakdown and have to go into hospital. The disturbance started with the patient's complaint that he could not drag himself away from the television screen where he was watching the Olympic Games. He felt forced, almost against his will to look at it until late at night. He complained that he was drawn into the hot climate of Mexico which made him feel that being there would make him swell. He was also compelled to look at the athletes, or wrestlers and weightlifters and felt he was, or ought to be, one of them. He asked me questions: Why have I to be an athlete? Why can't I be myself? He felt that this looking at television was like an addiction which he could not stop and which exhausted and drained him. At times he felt so strongly 'pulled inside the television' that he felt claustrophobic and had difficulty in breathing. Afterwards during the night he felt compelled to get up and see whether the taps of the washbasin in his flat were closed and whether the stoppers in the basin were blocking up the drainage. He was terrified that both his bath and the basin might overflow and eventually he confessed that he was afraid of being drowned and suffocated. I interpreted to him that after he felt that he was making progress and feeling separate from me he was suddenly overcome with impatience and envy of me and other men who were able to move about and were active. I suggested that it was the envious part which drove him into the identification with other men and myself in order to take over their strength and potency, and in this way the omnipotent part of himself could make him believe that he could be mature and healthy instantly. He agreed with the interpretation without any difficulty and started to speak very fast: he said he knew all this and was quite aware of it, but he also knew that this belief was quite false and that it was a delusion and he was angry at having to listen to a voice in him which was very persuasive and stimulated him to take over the mind and body of other people. I also interpreted to him that I thought that the threatening separation was stimulating his wish to be suddenly grown up and independent in order not to have to cope with the anxieties of being separate from me. He then told me that he was falling every night into a very deep sleep from which he could not easily awake in the morning and so he had arrived late for his session. He compared the feeling of being pulled into the television screen, which seemed to have become identified with the delusional object, to being pulled into this deep sleep. He now spoke fairly fluently and more distinctly and conveyed that he felt now more separate from me. He said he felt disgusted with himself for being a parasite and he also complained that the television experience and his bed were draining his life out of him, so that he had a strong impulse to smash both; he was glad that he had been able to control this in reality. I acknowledged his own observation that his looking at television and being pulled into a deep sleep were experienced by him as parasitical experiences where he felt he was getting into other objects. I pointed out that he felt angry with that part of himself which stimulated him to get inside external objects, the athletes representing me as a successful man who was travelling abroad during the break, and also into internal objects which were represented by his bed. I stressed that at first he felt he probably could control and possess these objects entirely when he got inside them, but very soon he felt enclosed and trapped and persecuted, which roused his wish to destroy the bed and the television screen which had turned into persecuting objects. I thought that his fear of being trapped and his anger related also to the analysis and the analyst. The patient's obsessions about the stoppers of the basin were also related to his fear of being trapped and drowned. It seemed that he had constantly to find out whether after his intrusion into objects he was trapped and was in danger of drowning and suffocating inside, or whether there was a hole through which he could escape.

Simultaneously with the projective identification related to the delusional television experience, the patient was violently pulled into relations to prostitutes. He explained to me that there was a part of him which persuaded him whenever he felt lonely or anxious that he needed to have a lovely big prostitute for nourishment and this would make him well. During the session he assured me that he realized the falsity of the voice, but in fact he very rarely could resist. He felt he wanted to get inside the prostitutes in an excited way in order to devour them, but after intercourse he felt sick and disgusted and convinced that he had now acquired syphilis of the stomach. The patient, during this session, many times asserted that he knew quite well the difference between reality and the delusional persuasion and he also knew what was wrong. But it was clear to me that in spite of this knowledge he was again and again put temporarily into a deluded state by a psychotic omnipotent and omniscient part of him which succeeded in seducing and overpowering the saner part of his personality and induced him to deal with all his difficulties and problems, including his envy, by projective identification. During the session, the saner part of the patient seemed to receive help and support from the analyst's interpretations, but he felt humiliated and angry that he could not resist the domination and persuasion of the psychotic part when he was left on his own. In attempting to examine the reason for listening so readily to the internal voice, I found that he was promised cure, freedom from anxiety and from dependence on myself. I was then able to interpret that the separation made him more aware of feeling small and dependent on me, which was humiliating and painful and increased his envy of me. By omnipotently intruding into me, he could delude himself that from one moment to the next he became grown up and completely all right and could manage without me.

I shall now briefly describe the relationship between ego splitting, projective identification and the persecutory anxieties related to these processes in this patient. On the following session he reported that he felt much better, but in the middle of the session he became very silent and then admitted with shame that he had been intensely anti-semitic some time ago for a period of over six months. He had regard the Jews as degraded people who were only out to exploit others in order to extract money from them in a ruthless way. He hated exploiters and wanted to attack and smash them for it. I interpreted that while he was aware that this happened in the past, he now felt awful towards me because after yesterday's session he had got rid of the greedy parasitical exploiting part of his self but had pushed it into me. He felt now that I had become his greedy exploiting self and this made him feel intensely suspicious about me. He replied that he feared that I must now hate and despise him, and that the only thing which he could do was to destroy himself or this hated part of himself. I interpreted his fear of my retaliation because when he saw me as a greedy, exploiting Jew he attacked and despised me, and feared that I would hate him because he believed I could not bear that he had pushed his own greedy self into me, not only as an attack but because he could not bear it himself and wanted to get rid of it. I suggested that it was when he felt that I could not accept his bad and hated self that he attacked himself so violently. In fact, the greatest anxiety during this session was related to violent attacks that were directed against his bad self which built up to a crescendo, so that he feared he would tear himself to pieces. He calmed down considerably after the interpretations.

The next session showed progress in relation to the splitting processes, followed in subsequent sessions by some experience of depression. In the beginning of the session the patient reported that he had some difficulty in getting up, but he was glad that he remembered a dream. In this dream he was observing a group of Olympic runners in a race on the television screen. Suddenly he saw a number of people crowding in on to the track and interfering with the race. He got violently angry with them and wanted to kill them for interfering and deliberately getting in the way of the runners. He reported that he had been looking at the television screen for only a short time the night before and had been thinking about the last session in which he had been afraid of damaging himself when he tried to cut off and destroy bad parts of himself. He now was determined to face up to whatever was going on in him. He had no associations to the dream, apart from the fact that the interfering people looked quite ordinary. I pointed out that in this dream he showed in a very concrete way what he felt he was doing when he seemed to be the parts of himself which he experienced as worming their way into the track in Mexico when he was greedily and enviously looking at television. In this dream it was quite clear that people representing him were not competing by running, but were simply trying to interfere with the progress of the race. I was then able to show him another aspect of the extremely concrete form of projection which did not only relate to the Olympic runners but to the analyst. I interpreted that he felt when the analysis was making good progress he experienced my interpretations and thoughts as something which he was watching with admiration and envy, like the athletes on television. He felt that the envious parts of himself actually could worm their way into my brain and interfere with the quickness of my thinking. In the dream he was attempting to face up to the recognition that these parts of himself actually existed and he wanted to control and stop them. I also related this process to the patient's complaints that his own thought processes were often interfered with and I related this to an identification with the analyst's mind which he often enviously attacked. Actually, the patient's co-operation during the last week had been very positive, which had led to considerable unblocking of his mind, so that a great number of his projective identifications and splitting processes had shown themselves clearly in the analysis and could be related to the transference situation. In the dream he had actually succeeded in what he announced he tried to do, namely, to face up to the processes by bringing them into the transference rather than attempting to destroy and get rid of them by splitting and projection. This also enabled him to face up to his acute fear of damaging both his objects and his self through his projective identifications. My interpretations seemed to diminish his anxiety about having completely destroyed me and my brain so that I could be experienced as helpful and undamaged, and for certain periods I was introjected as good and undamaged, a process leading gradually to a strengthening of the ego. One of the difficulties of working through such situations in the analysis is the tendency to endless repetition, in spite of the patient's understanding that very useful analytic work is being done. It is important in dealing with patients and processes of this kind to accept that much of the repetition is inevitable. The acceptance by the analyst of the patient's processes being re-enacted in the transference helps the patient to feel that the self, which is constantly split off and projected into the analyst, is acceptable and not so damaging as feared.

I want now to describe briefly a short depressive spell in the patient's illness which throws some light on his internal anxieties related to damage to objects and his self. A few days after the session I reported before the patient became increasingly concerned about injuries he believed he had done to other people, but most of all he was horrified about what was going on inside himself. For half an hour he experienced intense anxiety and reported that he was too frightened to look inside himself. Suddenly he saw his brain in a terrible state as if many worms had eaten their way into it. He feared that the damage was irreparable and his brain might fall to pieces. Despairingly he said how could he allow his brain to get into such an awful state! After a pause he suggested that his constant relations to prostitutes had something to do with the state of affairs. I interpreted that he felt that he had forced himself during the last weeks into people such as the prostitutes and the athletes and that he was afraid to see that damage outside. The damage to his brain seemed identical to the damage he feared he had done to external objects. He then began to talk about his brain as a particularly valuable and delicate part of his body which he had neglected and left unprotected. His voice sounded now much warmer and more concerned than ever previously, so I felt it necessary to interpret that his brain was also identified with a particularly valuable important object relationship, namely, the analysis and the analyst which represented the feeding situation to him. This he had usually displaced on to the prostitutes to whom he always went for nourishment. I gave him now detailed interpretations of the intensity of his hunger for me, his inability to wait and I described his impulses and the self which he had experienced as boring himself omnipotently into my brain which contained for him all the valuable knowledge which he longed to possess. Throughout the hour the patient felt great anxiety and almost unbearable pain because he feared he could not repair the damage. However he was clearly relieved through the transference interpretations which helped him to differentiate and disentangle the confusion between inside and outside, phantasy and reality. I think it was particularly the interpretations about my brain which showed him that I could still think and function, which both helped him to understand this very concrete phantasy in relation to his own thought processes and to relieve his anxiety about the damage he feared he had done to me.

In this case material I have tried to illustrate some of the processes of projective identification and ego splitting and the part they play in the psychopathology of psychotic patients.

SUMMARY

'Projective identification' relates first of all to a splitting process of the early ego, where either good or bad parts of the self are split off from the ego and are as a further step projected in love or hatred into external objects, which leads to fusion and identification of the projected parts of the self with the external objects. There are important paranoid anxieties related to these processes as the objects filled with aggressive parts of the self become persecuting and are experienced by the patient as threatening to retaliate by forcing themselves and the bad parts of the self which they contain back again into the ego.

In this paper I have discussed a number of processes related to projective identification which play an important part in psychotic patients. First of all, I am distinguishing between two types of projective identification: the projective identification used by psychotic patients for communication with other objects, which seems to be a distortion or intensification of the normal infantile relationship which is based on non-verbal communication between infant and mother; and secondly, the projective identification used for ridding the self of unwanted parts, which leads to a denial of psychic reality. As a third point I am discussing projective identification representing a very common transference relationship of the psychotic patient which is aimed at controlling the analyst's body and mind, which seems to be based on a very early infantile type of object relationship. My fourth point is projective identification used by the psychotic patient predominantly for defensive purposes to deal with aggressive impulses, particularly envy. The fifth point I am drawing attention to are those object relations of the psychotic patient in analysis where he maintains the belief that he is living entirely inside an object – the analyst – and behaves like a parasite using the capacities of the analyst, who is expected to function as his ego. Severe parasitism may be regarded as a state of total projective identification. I am also discussing the parasitical state which is related to living entirely in a delusional world. Sixthly, I am discussing the *psychoanalytic treatment* of the processes related to projective identification in the psychotic patient. Finally, I shall present case material of a schizophrenic patient in order to illustrate some aspects of projective identification and ego splitting.

Notes

1 When Edith Jacobson describes the defensive nature of the projective identification in her adult psychotic patients she stresses the projection of bad parts of the self into external objects in order to avoid psychotic confusions, in other words she sees the projective identification of the adult psychotic as the attempt to split off and project into a suitable external object those parts of the self which are unacceptable to the adult ego: the external object would then represent the patient's 'bad self'.

2 Dr Segal (1957) also stresses greater awareness and differentiation of the separateness between the ego and object in normal symbol formation. She thinks that symbolization is closely related to the development of the ego and the objects which occur in the depressive position. She emphasizes 'that symbols are in addition to other factors created in the internal world as a means of restoring, recreating, recapturing and owning again the original object. But in keeping with the increased reality sense, they are now felt as created by the ego and therefore never completely equated with the original object.'

3 The loss of the capacity for abstract and symbolic thinking of the schizophrenic patient, which leads on to very concrete modes of thinking, has been described by many writers such as Vigotsky, Goldstein and others. Harold Searles (1962) in his paper 'The Differentiation between Concrete and Metaphorical Thinking in the Recovering Schizophrenic Patient' suggests that the concrete thought disorders depend on the fluidity of the ego boundaries when self and object are not clearly differentiated.

In one of his cases he describes 'abundant evidence of massive projection, not only on to human beings around him but also on to trees, animals, buildings and all sorts of inanimate objects'. Only when ego boundaries gradually become firmly established through treatment can figurative or symbolic thinking develop. Searles' observations have a close relationship to my own observation that excessive projective identification, leading to fusion between self and object, always causes loss of the capacity for symbolic and verbal thinking.

4 It is of course important to differentiate between a patient's rejection of the analyst's bad handling or misunderstanding, which would repeat a bad feeding situation from the envious aggression of the child which occurs in a good setting. The latter is not only difficult for the primitive ego of the child to tolerate but creates a particularly difficult problem for any loving and caring mother.

References

Bion, W. (1962) *Learning from Experience*, London: Heinemann; paperback Maresfield; reprints, London: Karnac Books (1984).

Bion, W. (1965) *Transformations*, London: Heinemann; paperback Maresfield; reprint, London: Karnac Books (1984).

Klein, M. (1946) 'Notes on Some Schizoid Mechanisms', in M. Klein, P. Heimann, S. Isaacs and J. Riviere *Developments in Psycho-Analysis* (1952), London: Hogarth Press, 292–320; also in *The Writings of Melanie Klein*, vol. 3, 1–24.

Jacobson, E. (1954) 'Contribution to the metapsychology of psychotic identifications', in *Journal of the American Psychoanalytical Association*, vol. 2.

Jacobson, E. (1967) *Psychotic Conflict and Reality*, New York: International Universities Press.

Mahler, M. (1952) 'On Child Psychosis and Schizophrenia. Autistic and Symbiotic Infantile Psychoses', in *Psychoanalytic Study of the Child*, vol. 7.

Mahler, M. (1967) 'On Human Symbiosis and the Vicissitudes of Individuation', in *Journal of the American Psychoanalytical Association*, vol. 15, 4.

Meltzer, D. (1967) *The Psychoanalytic Process*, London: Heinemann.

Rosenfeld, H. (1964) 'Object Relations of an Acute Schizophrenic Patient in the Transference Situation', in *Recent Research on Schizophrenia*, Psychiatric Research Reports of the American Psychiatric Association.

Rosenfeld, H. (1965) *Psychotic States: A Psychoanalytic Approach*, London: Hogarth Press.

Rosenfeld, H. (1969) 'The Negative Therapeutic Reaction', in P. Giovacchini (ed.), *Tactics and Techniques in Psychoanalytic Theory* (1975), New York: Jason Aronson, vol. 2.

Rosenfeld, H. A. (1964) 'On the Psychopathology of Narcissism: A Clinical Approach'. *International Journal of Psycho-Analysis*, 45, 332–7. Reprinted in *Psychotic States*, 169–79, London: Hogarth Press.

Searles, H. F. (1962) 'The Differentiation Between Concrete and Metaphorical Thinking in the Recovering Schizophrenic Patient', in *Journal of the American Psychoanalytical Association*, vol. 10.

Segal, H. (1950) 'Some Aspects of the Analysis of a Schizophrenic', in *International Journal of Psycho-Analysis*, vol. 31, 268–78; also in *The Work of Hanna Segal* (1981), New York: Jason Aronson, 101–20.

Segal, H. (1957) 'Notes on Symbol Formation', in *International Journal of Psycho-Analysis*, vol. 38, 391–7; also in *The Work of Hanna Segal* and reprinted here, 160–77.

Index

Karnac Books

Retail Sales
118 Finchley Rc
London NW3 5F
VAT No: GB 238 75.. ..
Company Reg: 480031

020 7431 1075 www.kar

Projective Identific.	99
Encounters with Mela	99
Rosenfeld in Retrospect: Essa	26.99
TOTAL	77.97
TENDERED(CASH)	100.00
CHANGE(CASH)	22.03

Inc. VATCode(z)   0.00

12/2012 15:31 siobhan Ref:362876
C:4 shop (Goods Taken)